Edinburgh Bilingual Library (1)

PAUL VALÉRY
Le Cimetière Marin

THE GRAVEYARD BY THE SEA
Edited and Translated by
GRAHAM DUNSTAN MARTIN
Lecturer in French
University of Edinburgh

for the University Press
Edinburgh

© Graham Dunstan Martin 1971
EDINBURGH UNIVERSITY PRESS
22 George Square, Edinburgh

ISBN 0 85224 179 8

North America
Aldine Publishing Company
529 South Wabash Avenue, Chicago

Library of Congress
Catalog Card Number 70–115062

Set in 10/11 'Monotype' Barbou
and printed in Great Britain by
W & J Mackay & Co Ltd, Chatham, Kent

PREFACE

It is often said that translation is impossible. This is a statement that a translator must respect but is obliged to disregard. Clearly, the meticulous rime-scheme and complex interechoing of sounds characteristic of Valéry cannot be imitated in another language save at the expense of words and their especial overtones. On the other hand some type of formal metre is essential if the mood given by Valéry's rhythms is somehow to be suggested. The blank-verse pentameter, branded firmly into the consciousness of English speakers, is possibly a regular enough irregularity for this purpose. The translation of poetry compels a slightly different approach from that of prose: for it is expression rather than ideas that constitutes poetry; and it is the poet-translator's task to translate words rather than notions. I have tried to be as literal in my rendering as I could.

As for the Commentary which follows the Poem, I do not suppose that I have read all that has been written about *le Cimetière marin,* since I have not read all that has been written about Valéry; such a task would be impossibly large. Let me also apologize here and now for any unacknowledged borrowings I may have made from others. In this kind of endeavour, it is impossible to avoid repeating some of what has been already noted by such commentators as Walzer, Cohen, Palgen and Weinberg—it is indeed *essential* to repeat it. My excuse for offering yet another commentary is that nothing like all has yet been said, even in Walzer's admirable book, about *le Cimetière marin,* and more particularly about the very complex and ambiguous use of language in it. Indeed, since poetry is the purpose of the criticism of poetry, and a poem is always more than the sum of its meanings, all can *never* be said, and the critic must keep returning to the poem.

The text of the poem and of the author's remarks upon it which I have used is that of the *Œuvres* of Paul Valéry, Bibliothèque de la Pléiade, Gallimard, Paris, 1957.

I wish also to take this opportunity of expressing my gratitude to all those who have generously given me advice and criticism; and in particular to Professor A.J. Steele of Edinburgh University for much patient and stimulating counsel.

G.D.M.

Contents

The Graveyard by the Sea
Paul Valéry

I. The Poet

Paul Valéry was born at Sète on the French Mediterranean coast in 1871, of mixed Corsican and Italian parentage. He was educated, first at Sète, later at Montpellier, where he had the successful scholastic career which is, revealingly enough, not infrequent among French literary figures. After studying law for several years, he moved to Paris, and in 1895 entered the War Ministry. This despite some uncomplimentary opinions at his interview there. One interviewer reported that he was an 'esprit absolument nuageux, vulgaire décadent, un Paul Varlaine (sic) dont l'administration n'a que faire' [a mind absolutely in the clouds, a vulgar decadent, a Paul Varlaine (sic) whom the administration has no use for]. Later he took a post at the Agence Havas, where he remained for over 20 years. A calm bourgeois exterior to his life, one would say; yet his wife was related to the painter Manet, and Pau Casals played at his wedding.

For his intellectual life was eventful enough. The young Valéry became acquainted with several of the leading literary figures of his day. His early poetry was praised by Mallarmé. For a time it seemed that he might make a reputation for himself as a poet. But in the autumn of 1892 he passed through a severe emotional crisis. An unrequited love-affair, whose effects were all the more serious since it seems to have been of the cerebral variety, reinforced various doubts about his ambition to be a poet and a celebrity, and no doubt about his ability to be one. He resolved he would devote himself henceforth to meditation upon the workings of his own intellect.

He did not, however, give up frequenting literary circles. Indeed, he did not start attending Mallarmé's famous Tuesdays, at which that poet would hold forth to an admiring circle of such men as Gauguin, Odilon Redon, Yeats and Gide, until some time after this crisis. He even continued to write occasionally, although in prose.

It is not uncommon for the tyro poet to give up writing in his early twenties. But it is extremely rare for him to begin again in his forties, and to be immediately acclaimed a major poet. What was the reason for Valéry's extraordinary silence during these years? There is no simple answer. Perhaps his law studies and later his profession—a most unpoetic one!—made if difficult for him to achieve the poetic mood. But he was also intensely self-critical, indeed a perfectionist. He pinned up in his room in Paris a notice reading 'Méfie-toi sans cesse!' [Be always on your guard!]. His early poetry left him dissatisfied. It had indeed much technique but little is conveyed through it. As he confessed in a letter to Gide,[1] he doubted whether poetry could ever achieve the overpowering emotional effects of the music of, for instance, Wagner. He was overawed too by the example of Mallarmé: the thought of vying with this sort of perfection paralysed him. And lastly, his intellectual preoccupations during these years of silence were those of self-analysis, the attempt to define the workings of his own intellect in terms of relationships analogous to mathematics. And analysis, as Valéry himself realized, and as we shall see him implying in *le Cimetière marin*, is more often than not the enemy of creation. It was logical for one attracted to the ideals of the 'decadents', of course, to take this stand. To attempt to live within an ivory tower is to reject experience; and to reject experience is to become unable to transmute it.

It required an accident to start him writing again. In 1912 his friend André Gide suggested to the publishing house of Gallimard that they should approach Valéry for a collection of his early poems. For this volume, Valéry began to write an 'Adieu à la Poésie', and the task began to absorb him. The poem grew and grew; he worked on it for five years, and the rough notes for it cover some eight hundred pages. It was finally published as 'La Jeune Parque' in 1917, and was an immediate success with the poetry-reading public. The long silence was, for the moment, over: during the next few years he worked on the poems later to appear in the collection 'Charmes'. Among these was *le Cimetière marin*.

Fame and honours were showered upon the poet during the last 20 years of his life. He became president of the P E N club, was given the Légion d'Honneur, lectured in France, England, Italy, Belgium and Spain, was elected to the French Academy, and to the chair of Poetry at the Collège de France, and at his death in 1945 was given a State funeral. He was interred at Sète, in his own 'Cimetière marin', and his tomb bears an inscription quoted from that poem: O récompense après une pensée / Qu'un long regard sur le calme des dieux.

Valéry's poetry is an example of perfectionism taken to unusual lengths. It is perhaps difficult, as Auden says, to write poetry at all in the modern world. There is no longer any generally accepted formula for art; and there are no generally accepted truths to form its content. The artist is obliged to engage in an agonizing personal search, for the only valid universal standards are his own personal ones. But how to determine what is *really* one's own ? Valéry's long years of silence and self-investigation enabled him to give some kind of answer to this problem. The search for the essentially personal tempts him to reject such inessentials as the demands of the body, the emotions, the character, the intellect; one is left with pure consciousness of consciousness. But what could be more universal than this ? On the other hand, the actual matter of poetry, its physical body, so to speak, must be composed of words and rhythms, and without the 'inessential' body there would be no words or rhythms. Valéry's poetry consequently occurs in a state of tension between the inner self as it yearns for purity, and the demands of the senses, which are universals too in the sense that they are the common property of humanity. This is the poet's answer to the problem. It is a personal answer in that it constitutes a personal view of his situation between two opposing universals.

But there are further difficulties for the modern poet: poetry has moved further away from prose than ever before: our poets tend to avoid pure representation and description, as did Mallarmé, and Valéry after him; they shun the more ordinary prose means of moving the reader. The individual word and image carry an enormous weight of meaning. Naturally, as Eliot puts it,

Words strain,
Crack and sometimes break, under the burden,
Under the tension, slip, slide, perish,
Decay with imprecision, will not stay in place,
Will not stay still.[2]

In this situation, Valéry added further rigorous technical requirements of his own. The poem must scan according to a strict pattern, the words within it must echo each other according to a complex scheme. Of course this is to some extent the poet's means of replacing dead formulae by his own new ones. It is ironical that these new formulae resemble the old ones so closely, and that we nowadays consider any formula to be as arbitrary as none! But Valéry knew this: as he explained to his readers, he did not use these formulae because they were traditional, but because any limitation was in fact a strength. '. . . Des chaussures trop étroites nous feraient inventer des danses toutes nouvelles.' [If footwear were too tight, we should have to invent new dances.][3] Poetry must be difficult to write as well as to read. Valéry's rigorous technical requirements were aids to difficulty. They are also, as is the frequently rather rhetorical atmosphere of the finished product, a sort of tough casing within which words find it more difficult than usual to 'strain, crack . . ., slip, slide (or) perish'. It must not however be thought that this poetry suffers from that peculiar Mallarméan chill which makes the latter's work at first so difficult to approach. The intellect is always firmly in control; but the emotions are always firmly there to be controlled. This is especially evident in *le Cimetière marin*.

It would not, therefore, be too misleading to compare the poetry of Valéry with that of the seventeenth-century Metaphysicals in England or of the Spanish *conceptistas*, especially Góngora, despite his latinized diction. (Even here, there is some resemblance, in that Valéry often uses words of Latin origin in their Latin sense.) In all, there is equivalence between intellect and emotion. In all, conceits and preciosity express this equivalence. In all, the odd and personal is raised to the level of the universal. In all, it is upon the heart of a *thinking* man that the poem centres.

That a poet should be concerned with form and intellect as well as with his emotions (or with the subconscious) seemed strange to the surrealists and their disciples. A generation ago, in fact, Valéry's poetry looked like the end of a process. He was the last symbolist, perhaps also the last classicist. But since the last war, French poetry has been reverting to a more 'traditional' approach: Yves Bonnefoy, for instance, exercises considerable formal and intellectual control over his poems. And the thinking mind is very definitely present in the poetry of the younger generation. Freedom of form and deprecation of rational control do not, in fact, define modernism. There were good reasons for the abandonment of traditional form in some kinds of modern poetry: a desire to approximate to the rhythms of natural speech, the need to express rhythmically the modern attitude to the human mind as a complex, self-contradictory and often confused organism, and so forth. But, rhythms apart, Valéry's imagery reflects an entirely modern psychology: each image is complex and obscure: he does not reduce emotional and intellectual processes to statement and description. As for surrealist unreason, one can validate it without invalidating Valéryan reason. And in any case, the links between his images are most often not expressed rationally, but are suggested by association, echo and juxtaposition.

The above analysis should help to explain or rebut several of the objections which readers are liable to raise about the poetry of Valéry. Is he overrhetorical? The text of *le Cimetière marin* is thick with exclamation marks. But the charge of rhetoric (in its popular, derogatory sense) cannot properly be levelled at him. Effect, in Valéry, does not take precedence over content. If one had a pair of scales to weigh the words used by poets, his would turn out to be as heavy, as packed with meaning and implication, as anyone's! It is true that one feels that language in Valéry is raised 'above' the level of ordinary speech, as for instance when he apostrophizes the sea or the sky: Beau ciel, vrai ciel, regarde-moi qui change! [Look on me, sky of truth and beauty, me/The changeable!], or writes, in Stanza 10:

Fermé, sacré, plein d'un feu sans matière,
Fragment terrestre offert à la lumière,
Ce lieu me plaît . . .
[*Closed, sacred, full of immaterial fire,*
Fragment of earth wide open to the light,
This place appeals . . .]

Here, 'fragment' is written instead of 'morceau'—which would have given a more commonplace effect; and the adjective 'terrestre' is used instead of the more usual possessive ('fragment de terre'), so that the phrase sounds more 'elevated' in style—partly, no doubt, because it reminds us of similar substitutions of adjective for possessive in Latin.[4] The mounting rhythm of these two lines, each phrase longer than the last, so that the effect of an expected climax is achieved, adds to this 'elevated' effect, as does the order of the phrases: the subject, 'lieu', is held back to the beginning of the third line, to assist the sense of climax. An elevated style is a feature of symbolist poetry: it is characteristic, for example, of Mallarmé. But, despite those modern poets who prefer a style approaching the colloquial, there is a place for Valéry's approach *provided that* his words have sufficient strength to be used in this way, and that (when the poet shifts his tone—as he does frequently) there is no sense of bathos rendering both the higher and lower levels of his tone equally suspect. As for his words having sufficient strength, I hope to show in the commentary following the poem that they have enough suggestive force and resonance. As for shifts of tone, Stanza 17 contains an interesting example: the first four lines sustain a fairly lofty tone, culminating in the phrase: 'Chanterez-vous quand serez vaporeuse?' [When thou art vapour, wilt thou sing?], where the pronoun 'vous' has been left out, suggesting medieval poetry or the 'style marotique'. We then have an immediate drop into the matter-of-fact: 'Allez! Tout fuit!' [Come, come! The world is fugitive . . .] But this is not bathos: this is not the poet falling off his own pedestal: he is here deliberately puncturing high hopes and wishful thinking. In short, an investigation of the shifts of tone in Valéry, and of whether they are sufficiently controlled, will give an answer favourable to the poet. Finally, though the rhythms of Valéry's work often reproduce the rhythms of traditional verse, then so do the rhythms of the users of free verse, which is to some extent a redevelopment of such rhythms. Eliot observes: '[Free verse] was a revolt against dead form, and a preparation for new form or for the renewal of the old.'[5] And the 'free verse' of both Eliot and Laforgue gives an impression of rhythms shifting constantly away from, and back to, an underlying 'regular' metre. Both are masters of rhythm, but Valéry performs the perhaps even more difficult feat of refreshing the traditional types of form he utilizes. Rhythms in poetry are too subtle for metrical analysis to be very revealing, but one can point to the constantly shifting phrase-lengths within the ten-syllable line that he uses in *le Cimetière marin*[6] and to his own observations on the genesis of the poem, where it is clear that he took pains to 'compose' an over-all rhythmic structure.[7]

A more serious charge is that his concern with 'purity' is ultimately life-rejecting, and that he accomplishes the act of poetry in some sense against his own will. This, I think, is to underestimate the importance of the senses to Valéry, and even to misconstrue his position in relation to his (hypothetical) 'pure self'. He is not in the position of a Claudel or of a Baudelaire, seeking their absolute on the further side of the senses, so that their progress is from self to senses to absolute; and he often depicts the act of poetry as a regrettable descent from purity. But this is natural, since the 'pure self' is one of the two extremes between which he sees himself situated. It and his 'forêt sensuelle'[8] are the two opposing forces between which his poetry works. Neither would function without the other, as darkness could not be defined without light. Is his technique too studied? Studied, it certainly is. But to claim that it is overcareful is to make the mistake which we hinted at above, namely, to suppose that one cannot reach the heart via the intellect. The charge is one that only those who suffer from Eliot's 'dissociation of sensibility' would make.

In any case, the final answer to this last objection is present in the poetry itself. One of the gravest difficulties which the modern poet has to face is that while he needs to be obscure (for the intellect alone is not enough), he also needs to attract our immediate interest. The best of Valéry's poetry is instantly attractive, not usually because of its imagery (though *le Cimetière marin* is an exception to this), but because of the fascinations of its sound, the subtle balance of its rhythms and the complex interechoing of vowels and consonants. This is a mellifluous and carefully composed music which appeals directly to the senses. Here, we may fairly say, sensual appeal and purity of poetic intention unite.

II. The Approach

All interpretations are imperfect. What indeed would the notion of a perfect interpretation mean? And all are different. In Valéry's own well-known words,

> 'Mes vers ont le sens qu'on leur prête. Celui que je leur donne ne s'ajuste qu'à moi, et n'est opposable à personne. C'est une erreur contraire à la nature de la poésie, et qui lui serait même mortelle, que de prétendre qu'à tout poème correspond un sens véritable, unique, et conforme ou identique à quelque pensée de l'auteur.'[9] [My poetry has the meaning that one ascribes to it. The meaning *I* give it suits only myself, and cannot be used as an objection against that given it by anyone else. It is an error contrary to the nature of poetry, and one which would even be fatal to it, to claim that to every poem there corresponds a true, unitary sense consistent or identical with some thought belonging to its author.]

This statement accords with Valéry's threefold distinction of poetry into author's poem, poem as object, and reader's poem. The poem has in some sense ceased to belong to its author once it has been published, even once other eyes have fallen upon it. Such was the case with the *Cimetière marin* itself. In April 1920, Jacques Rivière visited Valéry, looking for material for the *Nouvelle Revue Française*; found him poring over *le Cimetière marin*, thinking of suppressing, altering and adding; read the poem, was delighted with it, and bore it off in triumph for his magazine. 'C'est ainsi que par accident fut fixée la figure de cet ouvrage' [It is thus, by accident, that the form of this work came to be fixed], wrote Valéry; for after this, the only alterations he made to the poem were in the order of some of the stanzas.

If, however, this seems an extreme position to take up, Valéry moderates it elsewhere: 'Les oeuvres de l'esprit, poèmes ou autres, ne se rapportent qu'à *ce qui fait naître ce qui les fit naître elles-mêmes* . . .'[10] [The creations of the mind, whether poems or anything else, are concerned only with producing what produced them in the first place . . .]. In other words, a poem is a machine for the reproduction of a state of mind,[11] The more successfully it achieves this task, the 'better' the poem. That is to say, there is, in principle, a state of mind to be recreated. Perhaps one can produce some concordance between these points of view by saying that any *reasonable* view of a poem is valid. Certainly the word 'reasonable' begs a great many questions, but I think it can be held to function as a notion, just as the notion of 'the reasonable man' normally does in courts of law—and, as in courts of law, the coherence of one's judgment on a poem and its correspondence to the fact of the poem may be held to be the ultimate test. Reasonable men may differ, but only within reasonable limits; and the amount of their differing should reflect various possibilities of interpretation inherent in the poem.

Valéry himself implies a similar view: for he continues: 'Sans doute, des divergences peuvent se manifester entre les interprétations poétiques d'un poème, entre les impressions et les significations ou plutôt entre les résonances que provoquent, chez l'un ou chez l'autre, l'action de l'ouvrage. Mais . . . cette diversité possible des effets *légitimes* d'une oeuvre, est la marque même de l'esprit. Elle correspond, d'ailleurs, à la pluralité des voies qui se sont offertes à l'auteur pendant son travail de production. C'est que tout acte de l'esprit même est toujours comme accompagné d'une certaine atmosphère d'indétermination plus ou moins sensible.[12] [No doubt different poetic interpretations of a poem can reveal divergent impressions and meanings, or rather resonances, effected by the work upon different individuals. But . . . this possible diversity of the *legitimate* effects of a work is the distinguishing mark of the mind. Besides, it corresponds to the plurality of ways open to the author during his work of creation. You see, every authentic act of the mind is always as it were accompanied by a more or less appreciable atmosphere of indeterminacy.]

An atmosphere of indeterminacy; and a plurality of ways. If these ways are still in some sense present in the poem, then divergent interpretations are inevitable; they are even to be desired (as our first quotation showed Valéry insisting). More, a reading of the poem which can in any way be held to be correct must take into account these divergencies, or it is not a poetic reading of the poem. For, 'chaque mot assemble un son et un sens. Je me trompe: il est à la fois plusieurs sons et plusieurs sens. . . . *Plusieurs sens*, car les images que chaque mot nous suggère sont généralement assez différentes et leurs images secondaires infiniment différentes."[13] [every word combines a sound and a sense. No, I am mistaken: there are at the same time several sounds and several senses . . . *Several senses*, because the images suggested by each word are usually fairly diverse and their secondary images infinitely diverse.] Valéry was well aware, before Empson, of the role of ambiguity in poetry. In fact he goes so far as to state that it is in (1) the interlocking of the sounds of the poem, (2) the ambiguities of its words, and (3) the interlocking of these, that poetry consists: it is these things that distinguish it from prose.

I propose, therefore, in the pages that follow, to study certain of the interlocking ambiguities of *le Cimetière marin*, and without seeking to do the impossible (for one can never hope to exhaust the sense of a poem, and its secondary images, as we saw Valéry suggesting above, are infinitely diverse), to study at least some of the crossroads which its images constitute.[14] I hope that the result will be more complete, and take fuller account of such 'crossroads' than previous accounts have done, and help to clarify Valéry's statement that, in a poetic mood, when we are temporarily inhabitants of 'the poetic universe', 'known things and beings' appear to us differently:

'Ils s'appellent les uns les autres, ils s'associent tout autrement que selon les modes ordinaires; ils se trouvent (permettez-moi cette expression) *musicalisés*, devenus résonnants l'un par l'autre, et comme harmoniquement correspondants.'[15]
[They evoke each other, they are connected quite otherwise than in the normal way; they become (if you will allow me the expression) *musicalized*, made resonant by each other, and harmonically correlative.]

NOTES

I. THE POET

1. 27 March 1891.
2. Eliot *Burnt Norton*, lines 149–53.
3. Valéry *Œuvres*, Pléiade vol. I, p. 1305.
4. It will be noticed that, in my translation, quoted here, I have written 'fragment of earth' rather than 'terrestrial fragment'. For I feel that Valéry's elevated language has sometimes to be a little flattened in English, a language which can sustain less comfortably the lofty rhetorical note.
5. Eliot *On Poetry and Poets* (London: Faber 1957).
6. Thus, *Ce toit tranquille, où marchent des colombes*, divides 4/6; *Entre les pins palpite, entre les tombes*, 6/4; *O pour moi seul, à moi seul, en moi-même*, divides 4/3/3; and so on.
7. See p. 86.
8. His 'sensual forest', i.e. the tangled world of the senses.

II. THE APPROACH

9. Pléiade, vol. I, p. 1509. One may compare Valéry's statement: 'Si j'ai fait le portrait de Pierre, et si quelqu'un trouve que mon ouvrage ressemble à Jacques plus qu'à Pierre, je ne puis rien lui opposer—et son affirmation vaut la mienne.' [If I have painted a portrait of Peter, and if somebody thinks that my work looks more like James than Peter, there is no objection I can make to him—and his assertion is as valid as mine.] Pléiade, vol. II, p. 557.
10. Vol. I, p. 1350.
11. 'Un poème est une sorte de machine à produire l'état poétique au moyen des mots.' [A poem is a kind of machine for producing the poetic state by means of words.] Vol. I, p. 1337.
12. *Légitimes:* my italics: clearly the notion of 'the reasonable man' is here implied: there is a certain range of effects outside which the reader's reaction would *not* be legitimate (Vol. I, p. 1350).
13. Vol. I, p. 1369.
14. 'Le fond de la pensée est pavé de carrefours.' (Vol. II, p. 69) [The depths of thought are paved with crossroads.].
15. Vol. I, p. 1320.

Le Cimetière Marin

Μή, φίλα ψυχά, βίον ἀθάνατον
σπεῦδε, τὰν δ᾽ἔμπρακτον ἄντλει μαχανάν.
PINDARE, *Pythiques, III.*

1 Ce toit tranquille, où marchent des colombes,
Entre les pins palpite, entre les tombes;
Midi le juste y compose de feux
La mer, la mer, toujours recommencée!
O récompense après une pensée
Qu'un long regard sur le calme des dieux!

2 Quel pur travail de fins éclairs consume
Maint diamant d'imperceptible écume,
Et quelle paix semble se concevoir!
Quand sur l'abîme un soleil se repose,
Ouvrages purs d'une éternelle cause,
Le Temps scintille et le Songe est savoir.

3 Stable trésor, temple simple à Minerve,
Masse de calme, et visible réserve,
Eau sourcilleuse, Œil qui gardes en toi
Tant de sommeil sous un voile de flamme,
O mon silence! . . . Édifice dans l'âme,
Mais comble d'or aux mille tuiles, Toit!

4 Temple du Temps, qu'un seul soupir résume,
A ce point pur je monte et m'accoutume,
Tout entouré de mon regard marin;
Et comme aux dieux mon offrande suprême,
La scintillation sereine sème
Sur l'altitude un dédain souverain.

The Graveyard by the Sea

1 This peaceful roof where doves are walking
  Pulses between the tombs, between the pines;
  Noonday the just composes out of fires
  The sea, the sea, for ever recommencing!
  After a thought, O then what recompense
  A long gaze at the gods' serenity!

2 How finely worked the flashing that consumes
  Many a diamond of invisible foam,
  How true the peace that seems to be conceived!
  A sun reposes over the abyss
  And, pure creations of an eternal cause,
  Time scintillates and Dreaming is to know.

3 Minerva's temple unadorned, sure treasure,
  Mass of calm and visible reserve,
  Haughty and pensive water, Eye concealing
  So much of sleep under a veil of flame,
  My silence! . . . Mansion in the soul, and Roof!
  Yes, golden summit of ten thousand tiles!

4 Temple of Time, in a single sigh resumed,
  To this pure pitch ascending, I attune
  Myself, surrounded by my gazing sea;
  As a supreme offering to the gods,
  This tranquil scintillation sows upon
  The altitude a sovereign disdain.

5 Comme le fruit se fond en jouissance,
    Comme en délice il change son absence
    Dans une bouche où sa forme se meurt,
    Je hume ici ma future fumée,
    Et le ciel chante à l'âme consumée
    Le changement des rives en rumeur.

6 Beau ciel, vrai ciel, regarde-moi qui change !
    Après tant d'orgueil, après tant d'étrange
    Oisiveté, mais pleine de pouvoir,
    Je m'abandonne à ce brillant espace,
    Sur les maisons des morts mon ombre passe
    Qui m'apprivoise à son frêle mouvoir.

7 L'âme exposée aux torches du solstice,
    Je te soutiens, admirable justice
    De la lumière aux armes sans pitié !
    Je te rends pure à ta place première:
    Regarde-toi ! . . . Mais rendre la lumière
    Suppose d'ombre une morne moitié.

8 O pour moi seul, à moi seul, en moi-même,
    Auprès d'un cœur, aux sources du poème,
    Entre le vide et l'événement pur,
    J'attends l'écho de ma grandeur interne,
    Amère, sombre et sonore citerne,
    Sonnant dans l'âme un creux toujours futur !

9 Sais-tu, fausse captive des feuillages,
    Golfe mangeur de ces maigres grillages,
    Sur mes yeux clos, secrets éblouissants,
    Quel corps me traîne à sa fin paresseuse,
    Quel front l'attire à cette terre osseuse ?
    Une étincelle y pense à mes absents.

10 Fermé, sacré, plein d'un feu sans matière,
    Fragment terrestre offert à la lumière,
    Ce lieu me plaît, dominé de flambeaux,
    Composé d'or, de pierre et d'arbres sombres,
    Où tant de marbre est tremblant sur tant d'ombres;
    La mer fidèle y dort sur mes tombeaux !

5 And as a fruit into enjoyment melts,
  Its form dissolving, dying in the mouth,
  Changing its absence into sweetness, here
  I breathe the elusive smoke I shall become,
  And to my incandescent soul the sky
  Sings alteration in the restless shores.

6 Look on me, sky of truth and beauty, me
  The changeable! For after all my pride,
  My singular but potent idleness,
  Now to this brilliant space I abdicate,
  Across the houses of the dead my shadow
  Passes, subduing me to its frail motion.

7 My soul exposed to the torches of the solstice,
  O admirable justice of the light,
  I yet sustain your pitiless attack,
  Render you, pure, to your primordial place:
  Look on yourself! . . . But to reflect the light
  Supposes a dark half always in shadow.

8 For me alone, to me, within myself,
  Close to the heart and at the poem's spring,
  Between abeyance and the pure event,
  I await the echo of my secret depths,
  A salt, sombre, sonorous well resounding
  An always future hollow in the soul.

9 And you, feigned captive of the leaves, and gulf
  Devouring these thin railings, do you know
  The mysteries that dazzle my closed eyes,
  What body drags me to its lazy end,
  What mind attracts it to this bone-dry earth?
  A spark within recalls my absent dead.

10 Closed, sacred, full of immaterial fire,
   Fragment of earth wide open to the light,
   This place appeals, commanded by its torches,
   A composition of dark trees, of stone
   And gold, with marble tremulous on shadow,
   And sleeping on my tombs the faithful sea.

11 Chienne splendide, écarte l'idolâtre!
    Quand solitaire au sourire de pâtre,
    Je pais longtemps, moutons mystérieux,
    Le blanc troupeau de mes tranquilles tombes,
    Éloignes-en les prudentes colombes,
    Les songes vains, les anges curieux!

12 Ici venu, l'avenir est paresse.
    L'insecte net gratte la sécheresse;
    Tout est brûlé, défait, reçu dans l'air
    A je ne sais quelle sévère essence . . .
    La vie est vaste, étant ivre d'absence,
    Et l'amertume est douce, et l'esprit clair.

13 Les morts cachés sont bien dans cette terre
    Qui les réchauffe et sèche leur mystère.
    Midi là-haut, Midi sans mouvement
    En soi se pense et convient à soi-même . . .
    Tête complète et parfait diadème,
    Je suis en toi le secret changement.

14 Tu n'as que moi pour contenir tes craintes!
    Mes repentirs, mes doutes, mes contraintes
    Sont le défaut de ton grand diamant . . .
    Mais dans leur nuit toute lourde de marbres,
    Un peuple vague aux racines des arbres
    A pris déjà ton parti lentement.

15 Ils ont fondu dans une absence épaisse,
    L'argile rouge a bu la blanche espèce,
    Le don de vivre a passé dans les fleurs!
    Où sont des morts les phrases familières,
    L'art personnel, les âmes singulières?
    La larve file où se formaient des pleurs.

16 Les cris aigus des filles chatouillées,
    Les yeux, les dents, les paupières mouillées,
    Le sein charmant qui joue avec le feu,
    Le sang qui brille aux lèvres qui se rendent,
    Les derniers dons, les doigts qui les défendent,
    Tout va sous terre et rentre dans le jeu!

11 Resplendent watchdog, keep your guard against
The idolater! When I, a solitary,
A smiling shepherd, pasture long my sheep,
The white mysterious flock of peaceful tombs,
Hold off the overprudent doves, the empty
Dreams, the quaint and prying seraphim.

12 Once here, the future is pure idleness.
The brittle insect scrapes at the dry grit.
All is consumed, destroyed, evaporated
Into the air, into who knows what stern
Essence. And life is vast, heady with absence,
And bitterness is sweet and the mind clear.

13 The dead lie blanketed and easy here,
Warmed by the earth, their mystery parched away,
While, up above, Noonday the motionless
Suffices to itself and thinks itself . . .
Complete diadem, capital of perfection,
In you I follow, am, the hidden change.

14 There is no other to contain your fears!
It is my doubts, repentances, constraints
That are the flaw in your great diamond.
But underneath their stifling night of marble
A shadow folk among the cypress roots
Are on your way already lingering.

15 They have dissolved into a dense absence,
Their human whiteness drunk by the red clay,
The gift of life has passed on to the flowers.
Where are the dead's familiar turns of speech,
Personal talents, individual souls?
The larva threads where tears used to form.

16 The shrill cries of girls teased and tickled,
The shining eyes and teeth, the moist eyelids,
The charming breast playing with fire, the blood
Glowing at their surrendering lips, the last
Favours, the hands defending them, it all
Goes under earth and back into the game.

17 Et vous, grande âme, espérez-vous un songe
    Qui n'aura plus ces couleurs de mensonge
    Qu'aux yeux de chair l'onde et l'or font ici ?
    Chanterez-vous quand serez vaporeuse ?
    Allez ! Tout fuit ! Ma présence est poreuse,
    La sainte impatience meurt aussi !

18 Maigre immortalité noire et dorée,
    Consolatrice affreusement laurée,
    Qui de la mort fais un sein maternel,
    Le beau mensonge et la pieuse ruse !
    Qui ne connaît, et qui ne les refuse,
    Ce crâne vide et ce rire éternel !

19 Pères profonds, têtes inhabitées,
    Qui sous le poids de tant de pelletées,
    Etes la terre et confondez nos pas,
    Le vrai rongeur, le ver irréfutable
    N'est point pour vous qui dormez sous la table,
    Il vit de vie, il ne me quitte pas !

20 Amour, peut-être, ou de moi-même haine ?
    Sa dent secrète est de moi si prochaine
    Que tous les noms lui peuvent convenir !
    Qu'importe ! Il voit, il veut, il songe, il touche !
    Ma chair lui plaît, et jusque sur ma couche,
    A ce vivant je vis d'appartenir !

21 Zénon ! Cruel Zénon ! Zénon d'Élée !
    M'as-tu percé de cette flèche ailée
    Qui vibre, vole, et qui ne vole pas !
    Le son m'enfante et la flèche me tue !
    Ah ! le soleil . . . Quelle ombre de tortue
    Pour l'âme, Achille immobile à grands pas !

22 Non, non ! . . . Debout ! Dans l'ère successive !
    Brisez, mon corps, cette forme pensive !
    Buvez, mon sein, la naissance du vent !
    Une fraîcheur, de la mer exhalée,
    Me rend mon âme . . . O puissance salée !
    Courons à l'onde en rejaillir vivant !

17 And you, fine soul, are you in hopes to see
     A dream without the illusive colouring
     This gold and water have for mortal eyes?
     Tell me: when thou art vapour, wilt thou sing?
     Come, come! The world is fugitive, my presence
     Porous, even divine impatience dies!

18 Gaunt immortality in black and gold,
     Consoler grimly wreathed in laurel, making
     Believe that death's a warm maternal breast,
     Sublime falsehood, consecrated fraud!
     Who does not recognize them and reject
     That empty skull, that everlasting grin!

19 Profound forefathers, empty-headed ghosts,
     Who under the weight of so much shovelled earth
     Are mingled with it and confound our steps,
     The real, the irrefutable gnawing worm
     Is not for you, asleep beneath the table,
     He lives on life, he never gives me rest!

20 Self-love, maybe, or hatred of myself?
     His secret hunger biting in so close
     That any name would suit him equally.
     No matter! For he sees, wills, thinks and touches,
     I am his meat and even on my couch
     I live through my belonging to his life.

21 Zeno! Cruel Zeno! Zeno of Elea!
     And have you pinned me down with your barbed arrow
     Vibrating, flying and which cannot fly!
     The sound engenders me, the arrow kills!
     Ah! the sun . . . For the soul a tortoise-shadow,
     Achilles at full stride and motionless!

22 No, no! . . . Stand up! Into successive time!
     Breathe, my lungs, the birth of the wind! Shatter,
     My body, this reflective attitude!
     A freshness, exhalation of the sea,
     Restores to me my soul . . . Salt potency!
     Let's run to the waves and be flung back alive!

23 Oui! Grande mer de délires douée,
    Peau de panthère et chlamyde trouée
    De mille et mille idoles du soleil,
    Hydre absolue, ivre de ta chair bleue,
    Qui te remords l'étincelante queue
    Dans un tumulte au silence pareil,

24 Le vent se lève! . . . Il faut tenter de vivre!
    L'air immense ouvre et referme mon livre,
    La vague en poudre ose jaillir des rocs!
    Envolez-vous, pages tout éblouies!
    Rompez, vagues! Rompez d'eaux réjouies
    Ce toit tranquille où picoraient des focs!

23 Yes! Immense sea, dowered with ecstasy,
   Rippling skin of panther, ruffled chlamys
   Holed with a myriad idols of the sun,
   Intoxicated with your own blue flesh,
   O Hydra free and absolute, who bite
   Your sparkling tail in tumult like a silence,

24 The wind rises! . . . Life calls to be attempted!
   The boundless air opens and shuts my book,
   Bravely the waves in powder from the rocks
   Burst! Take to your wings, dazzled pages!
   Break, waves! Break with delighted water
   This peaceful roof where sails were pecking!

Commentary on
The Graveyard by the Sea

Valéry's own account of the genesis of the poem is well-known. 'Quant au *Cimetière marin*, cette intention ne fut d'abord qu'une figure rythmique vide, ou remplie de syllabes vaines, qui me vint obséder quelque temps.'[1] [In the case of *le Cimetière marin*, this intention was originally no more than a rhythmic pattern, empty, or rather filled with meaningless syllables, which came to obsess me for a time.] Little by little, he states, theme, sound and sense developed out of this rhythmic pattern. This account has been questioned, notably by L. J. Austin,[2] who observes that Valéry is evidently inspired by Poe's description of his having composed *The Raven* on a basis of purely abstract considerations.[3] Austin then notes that Schiller made a similar claim about his own creative process,[4] and goes on to state the major objection to Valéry's account: how can there be a necessary causal link between 'purely formal considerations' and the subject of a poem? Austin admits that the preoccupations of *le Cimetière marin* are those that are closest to Valéry's heart—but this is to deny a direct causal link. He concludes that Valéry's account is therefore only an 'ideal' one, and points out that the poet himself qualifies it, saying that he perhaps merely 'dreams' that he discovers his work progressively.[5] (Poe too is said to have confessed the inaccuracy of his account of the genesis of *The Raven*, in conversation with the Philadelphia poet, Thomas Buchanan Read.)[6] Well, this may be so; and no certainty is possible; but with a poet so intellectually self-conscious as Valéry, it seems dangerous to raise doubt to the level of disagreement. Lawler, consequently, defends Valéry's statements,[7] observing that the poet was interested above all in the relation of images and ideas to the laws of the mind, that this led naturally to the situation presented to us in *le Cimetière marin* of the poet meditating in front of an 'eternal scene', and that prolonged meditation on the eternal elements of nature might well 'lead to the subject of death'. This still seems, however, to provide no explanation for the appearance of the first words and images of the poem out of a mere rhythmic pattern.

And rhythm may well be the most important factor. Poe's description of his composition of *The Raven* was of course known to Valéry. It had been translated by Baudelaire, and commented on enthusiastically by both himself and Mallarmé. It was, in short, a part of the poetic tradition to which Valéry belonged. Is one then to suppose that he is merely reiterating a hopeful ideal that accords with his own prejudice? I think not—or at least, not entirely. For there is an important difference between Poe's account and Valéry's: Poe claims that he 'prefer(s) commencing with the consideration of an *effect*', that 'no one point in (the) composition (of *The Raven*) is referrible either to accident or intuition', and that even the *rhythm* of the poem arose out of purely abstract and rational considerations. Valéry's starting-point, however, was neither considered nor rational: it was a rhythm which 'came to obsess' him. There seems no reason to doubt his account of this as a starting-point: we have already seen that Schiller has a similar account to give; we have the testimony of Eliot: '. . . a poem, or a passage of a poem, may tend to realize itself first as a particular rhythm before it reaches expression in words, and . . . this rhythm may bring to birth the idea and the image; and I do not believe that this is an experience peculiar to myself';[8] and Valéry himself reiterates his own statement elsewhere,[9] following it by a description of how on one occasion, while walking in the streets of Paris, he became so to speak 'inhabited' by a rhythm which seemed 'alien' to him, how a further rhythm added itself to the first, so that he had the impression of an 'act of grace' which had mistaken the individual it was meant for. He was assisting at the birth of a musical composition, but, being no musician, was incapable of writing it down or profiting from it.

It seems to be an experience, then, of the poet, that rhythms do have a creative function. And if they do, this must be of stimulating in some way the appearance of actual words to fill the 'empty rhythm'. Now this could indeed be a matter of accident: it is no doubt often pure chance that certain words appear at a given moment rather than certain others, or it can be a question of something the poet has recently seen or read. But it might at least be worth while speculating on the likely effects of an obsessive rhythm on the mind of a creative poet. It has often been observed that living is intimately linked with various rhythms: we walk or run, the heart beats, those patterns of the brain's functioning which the electroencephalograph reveals to us follow certain rhythmic patterns, and so forth.[10] Or consider the hypnotic effect of the rhythmic swinging of, say, the hypnotist's watch at the end of its chain, or of the rhythmic beat of Voodoo drums. We do not even have to look so far afield as this: the effect of dance-rhythms is to make us wish to join in and, as we say, 'express ourselves'. It might indeed be the case that the poet, gripped by an obsessive rhythm, feels equally the necessity of 'expressing himself', and that certain rhythms tend to crystallize and bring to consciousness words connected with his profoundest unconscious concerns. For this would tend to suggest why the rhythm was in fact obsessive.

This does not, however, involve us in supposing that certain verse-forms inevitably evoke certain types of subject, as Valéry himself seems to suggest when he mentions that the ten-syllable line 'bears some relationship to the line of Dante'.[11] Each poet is, after all, an individual. Each poem is also an individual moment. Its rhythms are not identical with its scansion, any more than the rhythms of a symphony are identical with its bar-lines: both bar-lines and metrical scheme are merely a way of imposing a basic and widely applicable pattern upon the subtle and unrepeatable rhythms of particular 'performances': they do not constitute the rhythm, they merely help to indicate it. Valéry might, in short, be giving a true account of the effects upon him of a particular 'obsessive' rhythm. All this, tentative though it is, leads me to think that we cannot reject his account out of hand, and that perhaps it is admissible for him to claim that *le Cimetière marin* had to become

> 'un monologue de "moi", dans lequel les thèmes les plus simples et les plus constants de ma vie affective et intellectuelle . . . fussent appelés, tramés, opposés. . . . Tout ceci menait à la mort et touchait à la pensée pure.' [a monologue

of 'myself', in which the simplest and most constant themes
of my emotional and mental life . . . should be called up,
interwoven and contrasted. . . . All of which led directly
to the subject of death and bordered upon pure thought.][12]
Pure thought was a constant concern of Valéry's and Death is
at the back of every human mind, is indeed a central condition
of our existence.

At the start of the poem the sun is poised in a noonday
southern sky above a calm sea. Between the two, midway, if
you like, between heaven and earth, stands the Cemetery of
Sète, high on its cliff. The midday sun is the divine, poised in
the centre of its heaven or in the centre of its eternity; the sea
reflects the sun, as a mind, or minds in general, can picture
the absolute—or as Man, 'made in God's image', is himself a
reflection of the divine; and the graveyard reminds us of
mortality. The scene is tranquil. The sun is at its solstice,
apparently still. Both sea and cemetery seem fixed in a change-
less stability which reflects that of the absolute itself. But
doubts begin to occur to the poet. Are the three terms of his
metaphor (sun= sea= cemetery) really equivalent?[13] There
are hints of darkness and movement under the sea's glittering
surface: i.e. there are such hints under the intellectual and
meditative purity of the conscious mind. He turns to consider
the graveyard: at least in *death* the human being is still and
changeless. But the promise of immortality is a mockery: we go
underground to immobility, but it is dark there too. Neither
in life nor death can we be one with the unitary brilliance of
the absolute. A last intellectual doubt strikes him: remembering
the paradoxes of Zeno, he asks himself 'Is movement perhaps
a mere illusion?' But the body answers for him: it moves, it
requires action. And the poem closes with the wind breaking
the sea into waves, and with the poet asserting the reality of
life and action. A new metaphor has been established: Man is
no longer to be equated with the immobile sun or the silent
cemetery, but only with the changeable and turbulent sea.

We are at the start given two points of reference by Valéry
himself, in the epigraph from Pindar: Μή, φίλα ψυχά, βίον
ἀθάνατον σπεῦδε, τὰν δ'ἔμπρακτον ἄντλει μαχανάν. That is,
'Do not, my soul, seek immortal life, but exhaust the field
of the possible.' The opposition between the absolute and the
mobile present has been stated.

1 Ce toit tranquille, où marchent des colombes,
   Entre les pins palpite, entre les tombes;
   Midi le juste y compose de feux
   La mer, la mer, toujours recommencée!
   O récompense après une pensée
   Qu'un long regard sur le calme des dieux!

This peaceful roof where doves are walking
Pulses between the tombs, between the pines;
Noonday the just composes out of fires
The sea, the sea, for ever recommencing!
After a thought, O then what recompense
A long gaze at the gods' serenity!

The 'roof' is the sea, which particularly from where we are
standing, in the Graveyard, high up on the cliffs, does appear
to slope up towards the horizon like a roof. The 'doves' are the
sails of boats. The calm sea 'palpitates', that is, glitters in the
sun with a gentle movement of wavelets. Since 'palpitate' is a
verb used properly of living things, one guesses that the sea
stands for something living. The pines are upright, the tombs
recumbent: the one is a symbol for life, the other for death,
and the sea is seen through them, so that life and death are
associated: 'in the midst of life we are in death'. The other
main element in the metaphor is expressed by the words
'Midi le juste'. 'Midi' is in part a metaphor for the sun, and it is
'just' perhaps because it divides the day into two equal halves,
because it is regular as a clock, and because it appears serene.
Justice ($\Delta \acute{\iota} \kappa \eta$) was also the doorkeeper of Eternity in Par-
menidean philosophy; and in the same way as 'palpite'
attached the sea to life, so the adjective 'juste' attaches the sun
to the divine, which is justice itself. The action of 'composing'
too is proper to artists and to a divine Creator. Thus the 'fires',
which are visually the glitter of sunlight on the waves, are
creations of the divine, or images of it, as Man is said to be
created 'in the image of God'. Against the backcloth of eternity,
these individual lives burn away like flames, but succeed each
other endlessly: the sea of life is 'toujours recommencée'. But
'composer' means not only to create but also to calm: divinity
sinks these restless individual lives in the peace of eternity.
    One asks whose is the 'regard'. It is the poet's contemplating

the scene; and it is also the sea reflecting the sky. The combining of these two notions in a single image gives us a further sense for the sea: it is also the poet's mind contemplating the absolute. The sea, then, is both personal and universal. As Valéry says himself of the beginnings of *le Cimetière marin*, 'je m'orientais vers un monologue aussi personnel, mais aussi universel que je pourrais le construire.' [I was moving towards a monologue as personal, but also as universal, as I could make it.][14] As for 'le calme des dieux', this is ambiguously that of the sea, the sky, the cemetery, or of all three. And the feeling of overall calm is underlined by the repetition of the idea in the words 'tranquille', 'composé', 'calme', and by numerous words that echo the sound of these three. A general atmosphere of peace is created both by sense and sound.

But the calmness of the scene, though apparently total, includes elements of at least potential instability. This suggestion is given by the words 'palpite' and 'recommencée'. 'Après' too suggests that something different from this calm has gone before. So does 'une pensée', meaning a thought or a statement of thought. This is a human action, and forms an implied contrast with 'le calme des dieux'. The 'thought' might be the poet's poem, or an image in it, or the assemblage of images he is now contemplating. He has achieved a moment of rest in contemplation of his symbol and of the divine peace for which it stands. This moment of rest is the 'recompense' for his thought. Rightly, the two words 'récompense' and 'pensée' echo each other.

2   Quel pur travail de fins éclairs consume
    Maint diamant d'imperceptible écume,
    Et quelle paix semble se concevoir!
    Quand sur l'abîme un soleil se repose,
    Ouvrages purs d'une éternelle cause,
    Le Temps scintille et le Songe est savoir.

How finely worked the flashing that consumes
Many a diamond of invisible foam,
How true the peace that seems to be conceived!
A sun reposes over the abyss
And, pure creations of an eternal cause,
Time scintillates and Dreaming is to know.

The image at the start of the second stanza is of a cut diamond occupied, taken up, or filled (for such are some of the Latin senses of the verb 'consume') by its faceting (i.e. the 'travail de fins éclairs'). From a height these diamonds of foam cannot individually be seen. There is another sense of 'consume' too: we can take it as meaning 'consume, burn away', and we have then (1) a repetition of the image of the sea composed of fires, (2) the suggestion that these fires are blended into the overall glitter of sunlight on the sea, and (3) the implication that individual lives are being burned away in the totality of a divine process. For such a process 'pur travail' is an apt image. Thus, in the last line of the stanza, 'le Temps scintille', i.e. human lives are seen as an illusory flicker in the steady candle-flame of eternity. The poet is still lost in admiration of this eternity: he exclaims 'quelle paix semble se concevoir!' ['what peace seems to conceive itself' i.e. both 'thinks itself' and 'produces itself']. (Cf. Stanza 13.)

But there is a faint doubt. It only *seems* to conceive itself. Is this because one knows that the sea is never in fact still, for the individual diamonds of foam are there, though imperceptible? Is the peace itself in some way an illusion?

But we have not exhausted this image yet by any means. The sea is also the mind; and, like the mind, is complex, full of 'fins éclairs', its individual thoughts diamonds of foam at present indistinguishable in a mood of peaceful contemplation of the absolute. But once more we underline 'seems', and wonder if the mind is ever really still either. At the moment it seems to be contemplating itself—a key notion of Valéry's, to which we shall return later in the poem. And the equation of sea with mind leads one to suppose that the 'pur travail' of line 1 is also the apparent perfection of a work of art built out of mental labour. For 'travail', like 'work' in English, means not only the process of working, but also the finished work. So once again the image stands for something personal as well as something universal: for the artist's personal admiration for his art, as well as for Man's admiration of the absolute.

'L'abîme' introduces the first hint of darkness into the picture. There are depths of space between the sun and us, there are depths under the sea, there are the depths of the universe itself. But the word seems contextually rather surprising, so that the mind leaps to its general sense as well as to any particular applications it might have: so, metaphysically, the divine (ultimate reality) is supported by nothingness (the delusory world of appearances). But the image here is more impressive than this explanation would suggest, as successful images are always more impressive than any statement about them could possibly be. The suggestion of emptiness and of depth in the word foreshadows an aspect of the scene to which the poet is shortly going to turn his attention—the dark substructure beneath this picture of reigning brightness.

'Ouvrages purs' is no doubt either in apposition to 'Temps' and 'Songe' in the next line, or to 'soleil' and 'abîme' in the previous one. All are the work of the divine (which is the First Cause and eternal, hence an 'eternal cause'). 'Le Temps scintille' describes the flicker of light on the waves, and the flicker of passing time, each moment going out like a light, but followed by another lighting up. As for 'le Songe est savoir', one can paraphrase thus: 'This kind of contemplation is the only true knowledge', if one keeps in mind the overtones of the French word 'songe' (dream), which by its connexion with 'songer' implies thought, dreamy, contemplative, or deep and careful. The 'thought' of Stanza 1 has been re-echoed, as also the poet's 'work' in Stanza 2.

The poet's admiration for scene and situation reach their pinnacle in the next two stanzas:

3 Stable trésor, temple simple à Minerve,
Masse de calme, et visible réserve,
Eau sourcilleuse, Œil qui gardes en toi
Tant de sommeil sous un voile de flamme,
O mon silence! . . . Edifice dans l'âme,
Mais comble d'or aux mille tuiles, Toit!

Minerva's temple unadorned, sure treasure,
Mass of calm and visible reserve,
Haughty and pensive water, Eye concealing
So much of sleep under a veil of flame,
My silence! . . . Mansion in the soul, and Roof!
Yes, golden summit of ten thousand tiles!

The sea is seen here as the mind: it is the temple of Minerva, goddess of wisdom; it is an 'édifice dans l'âme'; its surface is compared to a vast eye—and the senses are, so to speak, the outer surface of the human mind. But also the eye is an image for the mind itself, which 'looks' and 'sees'.[15]

The first line has an interesting and typically Valéryan interechoing of sounds: 'Stable trésor, temple simple . . .' 'Stable' reiterates the idea of calm, as 'resérve', 'garde' and 'silence' do later in the stanza. 'Trésor' seems even more golden in French than 'treasure' does in English; for its last syllable, '-or', is the French for gold (a word repeated later in the stanza). All this assists the visual image of the golden glitter of sunlight on the water, but the riches referred to are also the riches of the mind. A similar double reference is present in 'réserve': both sea and mind are, in different senses, a sort of 'reservoir'. Temples too contain riches, are associated in our minds with rich decorations, but the adjective 'simple' and the association with Minerva make one think of the uncluttered purity of line of such ancient temples as (Minerva's) Parthenon. Hence the paradox of 'simple treasure', an appropriate image for the riches of the mind.

The alliterations of the first line, however, do not only echo each other, but also those in the preceding stanza: 'Le Temps scintille et le Songe est savoir.' And 'temple' echoes 'temps'. We have thus a definite link between the two main areas of meaning for which the sea stands. Time (to which life is bound) and the temple of the mind are here associated. The sea stands for both the mind and life.

The succession of metaphors describing the sea in this stanza are ambiguous too. 'Masse de calme' means both a calm mass, which the water literally is; and, metaphorically, an enormous calmness, weighty and solid, which describes the present state of the poet's mind. 'Réserve' links with the second notion, for it means not only a 'reserve or reservoir of water' but also 'guardedness, caution'; which in turn links up with 'O mon silence!' It is 'visible' in at least three senses: (1) it is visibly reserved; (2) it is in fact being looked at; (3) it is an Eye in the next line, so is capable of sight (which is one of the Latin senses of the word). 'Sourcilleuse' is a particularly suggestive word. Some of its reasons for being used are (1) because the water is compared to an eye, (2) because the sea is deep and seems to slant up to the horizon like a roof, and hence is lofty, (3) because the poet's mood is lofty or haughty, (4)

because it reminds one of 'soucieuse' (concerned or worried),
and (5) because the poet is frowning in concentration. The
'veil of flame' in the next line is the blaze of sunlight on the
surface of the water and the blaze of the absolute in the poet's
mind; the 'sleep' refers at once to the depths of the sea and to
the depths of the mind. The depths of the water are compared
to sleep primarily because they are dark and at rest. But there is
a profound psychological association between water and
sleep, water and dreams, water and the subconscious, due per-
haps to the state of the child in the womb, protected by the
amniotic fluid, to the lulling of a child asleep by rocking it, as
by a gentle motion of water, and to the sensation of floating
that sleep sometimes gives. As for the associations between
sleep and the depths of the mind, there are the images that
occur to us when we dream, and the way that images and ideas
could be said to 'be asleep' before they become conscious—
but of this, more will be said when we come to Stanza 8.
Hence, with the exclamation 'O mon silence!', Valéry is
addressing his own mind, its potentialities, its unconscious
depths, its present state of contemplative silence. The sea is
now not only a roof because it looks like one, but because,
standing for the mind, it crowns the building of the body, and
is in fact quite literally positioned above the body. The
'thousand tiles' are the sea's myriad waves, and, in so far as
they refer to the mind, its myriad neurons or its myriad ideas.

The word 'édifice' in line 5 does more than simply support
the image of the sea as roof and temple, for it reminds one of
'aedificare', to build. (The word is derived from 'facere' and
'aedes', which meant 'building' and often specifically 'temple'.)
In other words, there is a hint here of the *process* which built up
this present state of mental ecstasy. This reinforces previous
hints, such as 'pur travail de fins éclairs', 'pensée' in Stanza 1,
'sommeil' and 'réserve'; and links with the idea of 'altitude' in
Stanza 4. It is only the *surface* of the sea that reflects the sun;
it is only at the surface of the mind that this intellectual ecstasy
occurs: for this is the only area of the mind that 'reflects' (the
word is nowhere used by Valéry in this poem, but the process
is repeatedly described). Beneath this brilliant surface lie the
obscure workings of the mind (as we shall see the poet describ-
ing in Stanzas 7 and 8): it is they that 'build' the 'edifice'.
And building is ordering and organizing. Once again, the hint

of a process appears in the background of the apparently changeless present; only in certain privileged moments does the mind reach this pitch of magnificence ('comble d'or'), achieve the splendid simplicity of Athene's Temple.

4 Temple du Temps, qu'un seul soupir résume,
  A ce point pur je monte et m'accoutume,
  Tout entouré de mon regard marin;
  Et comme aux dieux mon offrande suprême,
  La scintillation sereine sème
  Sur l'altitude un dédain souverain.

Temple of Time, in a single sigh resumed,
To this pure pitch ascending, I attune
Myself, surrounded by my gazing sea;
As a supreme offering to the gods,
This tranquil scintillation sows upon
The altitude a sovereign disdain.

'Temple' and 'Time' were previously linked by sound. Here the idea of a 'Temple of Time' becomes specific. The reference of the phrase is highly ambiguous. On the one hand the Temple of Time is, beautifully and aptly enough, the cemetery through which the poet is climbing ('A ce point pur je monte . . .'). On the other, it repeats the language of the last two stanzas, and hence refers to the sea, and through them to the mind and to life. The human mind is a temple of time in that it is temporality's highest achievement, and is also at the mercy of time, and so is petty, brief and mortal. And life is a temple of time in that it is a phenomenon of time, it is where time works, acts and lives. The phrase 'qu'un seul soupir résume' is even more obscure. This is an example of what Empson calls 'ambiguity by vagueness'. A sigh can be occasioned by regret or by aspiration. 'Résume' can be taken in its normal French sense of 'sums up' or 'summarizes'; but also in a Latin sense: 'recovers, renews, restores'. In this second sense of 'résume', a sigh restores to the poet an awareness of temporality and eternity. In the first sense, eternity is glimpsed in the moment sufficient for a single sigh; and thus a sigh *for* the passage of time. In any case the phrase gives us another glimpse of the vital substructure: contemplative thought depends upon conscious mental activity, unconscious processes, emotions, and ultimately upon physical processes. And there is a hint of the opposition between the absolute and ourselves: it is changeless, but we are bound to time.

In the next line, 'A' depends upon both 'monte' and 'm'accoutume': they are hence linked more closely: the poet's accustoming himself to 'ce point pur' *constitutes* an increase in exaltation. What is the 'point pur'? Firstly, it is the cemetery through which the poet is climbing; secondly, the singular 'purity' of his state of mind; thirdly, the lofty pitch of his contemplation of the divine. The phrase expresses the difficulty of reaching such a pitch of exaltation (for he has to climb), and its strangeness to a human mind (for he has to accustom himself to it). He is 'entouré de (son) regard marin': for (1) he is looking at the sea, (2) the sea (which is Eye and Mind) is looking also; but since the sea can be his own mind, we have also (3) mind contemplating itself. One must give special force to the word 'marin': this is a special kind of 'look': his mind is at the moment compared to the sea reflecting the glory of the divine, a privileged state. This state is described further in the next three lines: it involves disdain to temporality, which could be the time-bound human being's supreme offering to the Gods. 'La scintillation sereine' causes this; for it is the flicker of passing time; and is the reflection of the divine in the mind. It is a 'sovereign disdain' because it is supreme, regal, and hence connected with the divine. 'L'altitude' means partly height. The sea, a 'roof', appears to be high up; the mind is in a privileged state. In Latin, however, the word meant depth as well as height. The sea is high and deep; the mind is high, and deep, and below the divine. And at this moment, the hidden depths of mind and sea are despised: a state of mental bliss is preferred to the dark and troubled workings of the mind that has achieved this state.

The ultimate pitch of admiration for the mind in its contemplation of divinity, and for that divinity itself, has now been reached. As if by reaction, and a natural human reflex, the poet is about to turn his attention to the human condition. Indeed, he has already by implication done so, for the word 'suprême' means in its Latin and Mallarméan sense, 'last' Man's last offering to the absolute, his last sacrifice, is his own death, after which he will be one with eternity, despising his

past mortal condition. But at the same time, disturbing over-
tones are produced by these telescoped senses of 'suprême': for
they equate the poet's contemplation of the divine while he is
still alive, with death.

5 Comme le fruit se fond en jouissance,
Comme en délice il change son absence
Dans une bouche où sa forme se meurt,
Je hume ici ma future fumée,
Et le ciel chante à l'âme consumée
Le changement des rives en rumeur.

And as a fruit into enjoyment melts,
Its form dissolving, dying in the mouth,
Changing its absence into sweetness, here
I breathe the elusive smoke I shall become,
And to my incandescent soul the sky
Sings alteration in the restless shores.

The language used for death is at first consoling, even alluring:
'jouissance . . . délice . . . le ciel chante . . .' The fruit melting
into sweetness is an image for the soul, at death, accepting
blissful annihilation into a Nirvana. Weinberg points to the
appropriateness of the sensuality here, and comments that
Man's refusal to discard the sensual will lead Valéry to his
ultimate rejection of this view of death—or rather, I should
say, the only form that acceptance of death *can* take is making
death itself appear pleasantly sensual. Once this picture of
death is rejected, as it will be in Stanzas 15–17, death itself
will be rejected too.

   In this connexion one notes the ambiguity of 'l'âme consu-
mée'. 'Consumed' means (as in Stanza 2) 'taken up with
eternal light'; but also 'destroyed, burnt away' (transformed
in fact into smoke as in the previous line). The image works in
two opposite directions: on the one hand a mystical bliss is
suggested; on the other, the death, not merely of the physical
man, but of the soul itself. An idea typical of Valéry: in 'Note
et Digression' he writes: '[Léonard de Vinci] songe:. . .l'âme,
quoique *chose divine*, ne se sépare qu'avec les plus grandes
peines de ce corps qu'elle habitait. "Et je crois bien, dit
Léonard, que ses larmes et sa douleur ne sont pas sans raison…"

Il suffit de considérer l'ombre énorme ici projetée par quelque idée en formation: la mort, interprétée comme un désastre pour *l'âme*!' [Leonardo da Vinci muses: It is only with the greatest distress that the soul, although a *thing divine*, separates from the body it inhabited. 'And I believe,' says Leonardo, 'that its tears and its grief are not without reason.'. . . One need only consider the enormous shadow cast here by an idea in process of formation: death, interpreted as a disaster *for the soul*!]][16] It is clear from the context that Valéry agrees: death *is* a disaster for the soul.

So far, this attitude of his has only been hinted at. But some part of our attention has now been directed to the element of change in human life: the 'rives' in the last line of this stanza are perhaps boundaries between life and death. And, in any case, the peaceful sea has now begun to move.

6 Beau ciel, vrai ciel, regarde-moi qui change!
   Après tant d'orgueil, après tant d'étrange
   Oisiveté, mais pleine de pouvoir,
   Je m'abandonne à ce brillant espace,
   Sur les maisons des morts mon ombre passe
   Qui m'apprivoise à son frêle mouvoir.

   Look on me, sky of truth and beauty, me
   The changeable! For after all my pride,
   My singular but potent idleness,
   Now to this brilliant space I abdicate,
   Across the houses of the dead my shadow
   Passes, subduing me to its frail motion.

And an opposition is born between the changing individual man and the changeless, eternal absolute. The sky, heaven, is 'beautiful and true', both attributes of the divine. The poet is still, however, reconciled to this situation: he 'abandons himself' in line 4, he accepts the thought of his death in line 5. These lines do not only mean acceptance of death in the future; they also, and most effectively, imagine that death in the present. 'Ce brillant espace' is the sky or the cemetery-ground, or the sea filled with the light of eternity, or at once all of these. The ambiguity serves to equate the various motionless states here described: sea (mind), sky (the absolute) and cemetery (death). And there are overtones of emptiness in the word 'espace': the light is blinding, but the atmosphere rarefied.

The last two lines have a double sense: his real-life shadow passes across the tombs, and he is 'tamed to its frail movement', i.e. reminded that he is mortal, reduced to his human proportions, reconciled to the idea of death. Secondly, his Shade is wandering among the houses of the dead, the tomb, Hades; and he is reduced to the proportions of a ghost. No movement could be frailer, slighter, than that of a shadow or a ghost.

7 L'âme exposée aux torches du solstice,
   Je te soutiens, admirable justice
   De la lumière aux armes sans pitié!
   Je te rends pure à ta place première:
   Regarde-toi!... Mais rendre la lumière
   Suppose d'ombre une morne moitié.

My soul exposed to the torches of the solstice,
O admirable justice of the light,
I yet sustain your pitiless attack,
Render you, pure, to your primordial place:
Look on yourself!... But to reflect the light
Supposes a dark half always in shadow.

The exposure of the soul to 'the torches of the solstice' reminds one of the 'soul consumed' in Stanza 5. This exposure is both delicious and dangerous. 'Solstice' places the scene at midsummer: the sun is at its closest to our hemisphere. At this stage in its movement, it seems to hang at midday at its culminating point, to rise for several consecutive days at the same point on the horizon, and to have the same declination. It is thus apparently motionless; and the Latin origin of the word 'solstice' underlines this illusion, formed as it is from 'sol' and 'stare'. The word gives us, then, the ideas of culmination, of a peak of heat and light, and of immobility. The poet has become a perfect reflector of the sun ('Je te soutiens, admirable justice'). The word 'admirable' implies admiration, contemplation, and, by its connexion with words like 'miroir', reflection. 'Je te soutiens' and 'Je te rends pur' mean a similar perfect reflection of the absolute, and, in another sense, that the poet is not balking at giving the absolute its due, at admitting its purity and primacy. The exclamation 'Regarde-toi!' echoes 'regarde-moi' in Stanza 6: the absolute is asked to look at its own reflection in the poet's mind. Man and sun, according to Weinberg, appear to have been merged. But because of the depths in sea and man, this merging is about to be shown to be illusory.

For 'rendre la lumière/Suppose d'ombre une morne moitié.' The image is that of a moon, one half in shadow, or of a body in the sun, one half in shadow; or of a mirror, which needs a 'dark' backing. For the etymology of 'suppose' also suggests the meaning 'under-puts'. The necessity of darkness for reflection is suggested to us by the conviction carried by the sounds. Most of the consonants in this last line are labials, most of the vowels o's and u's. Hence the darkness associated with the words 'ombre' and 'morne' seems to cast its shadow over the whole line. This is a statement which can be very accurately applied to the mind: it has its own dark area, the unconscious, and depends for existence upon the physical. Only in a state of ethereal intellectuality, of a renunciation of life similar to that of Valéry's M. Teste, does this 'darkness' seem to be abolished. It can also be accurately applied to human life: for we all carry our mortality around with us, like the shadow falling across the tombs in the previous stanza. Moreover, our physical mortality is the condition without which our apparently spiritual elements cannot exist. Their existence pre 'supposes' the existence of the mortal body. The last line and a half of this stanza consequently mark an abrupt fall from exaltation into an awareness of the realities of the human condition. For where is the poet to look now for his absolute of contemplation? Only by abandoning the unconscious, the physical, the 'darkness' in himself, can he find it within his own living mind.

8 O pour moi seul, à moi seul, en moi-même,
   Auprès d'un cœur, aux sources du poème,
   Entre le vide et l'événement pur,
   J'attends l'écho de ma grandeur interne,
   Amère, sombre et sonore citerne,
   Sonnant dans l'âme un creux toujours futur !

For me alone, to me, within myself,
Close to the heart and at the poem's spring,
Between abeyance and the pure event,
I await the echo of my secret depths,
A salt, sombre, sonorous well resounding
An always future hollow in the soul.

The human condition is, first of all, the poet's condition. He looks into himself and explains how his inner darkness appears. The reiterated 'moi's and 'seul's at the beginning of the stanza are in part a refusal to look heavenwards any more, in part a denial that any of the mental processes about to be described could be experienced by the absolute, in part an acceptance of the individual's fundamental solitude.

One might well ask why the poet is here writing poetry about writing poetry. For this is what we have here. Valéry's description in these lines of an inner mental process is much the same as his description of what he calls the 'Implex' in 'L'Idée fixe'. According to Valéry in this dialogue, the 'Implex' is not at all the same sort of thing as the subconscious or unconscious: it is (I paraphrase) a sort of complex of associated ideas. We proceed from idea to idea, hunting the one we need; we do not yet know it, but we recognize it once it appears to us, apparently 'ex nihilo'.[17] Now, according to Valéry, this process is not peculiar to the poet, but is common to most intellectual activity. So once again, this use of the example of the poet's personal experience has a universal validity. Discussing the same problem in 'Variété', and specifically from the point of view of the poet at work, he says: 'Il semble qu'il y ait dans cet ordre des choses mentales, quelques relations très mystèrieuses *entre le désir et l'événement.*' [It seems that, in this order of mental phenomena, there are certain very mysterious relationships *between the desire and the event.*][18] Here too, the poet 'attend l'écho de (sa) grandeur interne...Entre le vide et l'événement pur...' [awaits the echo of (his) inner greatness . . . between the void and the pure event . . .] The emotions are closely involved ('Auprès d'un coeur'), and 'echo' is exactly appropriate to the situation: the depths of the mind constitute an 'Amère, sombre et sonore citerne'—sonorous words, and rightly so! For in this mysterious area of the mind, words are associated with words through similarity of sound as well as meaning. Thus here, 'citerne' appears to contain the word 'terne' (dull, leaden), and reminds us of 'réserve' (Stanza 3); and 'amère' (bitter) appears to contain 'mer'. The lines describe not merely this situation, but also the mental effect of a line of genuine poetry: the words echo each other in both meaning and sound, and stimulate further echoes. The 'creux toujours futur' is, from the poet's point of view, the echoing hollows of the mind, empty because echoing, empty also because before each new word appears it is 'always future', never more than potential. It is clear why these mental depths should be 'dark': nothing can be seen in them, and they are mysterious. But is there a further meaning to the word? Why, for instance are they 'bitter'? It is partly due to their equation with the sea, no doubt; but perhaps there is also an overtone of human regret. There may be a connexion between 'creux' and the hollowness of vaults. And why does the next stanza immediately continue with the theme of death? 'Futur' after all, necessarily implies temporality. The poet's look at his own mental processes makes him aware that they are bound to time as much as he is himself.

So here he is not only talking about the mental process of creating poetry, but is suggesting one of the 'implexes' involved, one of the complexes of feelings and ideas contained in the caverns of the mind, namely death. One can begin to see why, in his remarks on the composition of *le Cimetière marin*, Valéry said 'Tout ceci menait à la mort et touchait à la pensée pure.' [All this led directly to the subject of death and bordered upon pure thought.][19]

9 Sais-tu, fausse captive des feuillages,
   Golfe mangeur de ces maigres grillages,
   Sur mes yeux clos, secrets éblouissants,
   Quel corps me traîne à sa fin paresseuse,
   Quel front l'attire à cette terre osseuse?
   Une étincelle y pense à mes absents.

And you, feigned captive of the leaves, and gulf
Devouring these thin railings, do you know
The mysteries that dazzle my closed eyes,
What body drags me to its lazy end,
What mind attracts it to this bone-dry earth?
A spark within recalls my absent dead.

Valéry now turns and addresses the sea, 'golfe mangeur de ces
maigres grillages' because the iron railings surrounding each
tomb are corroded by the sea-air, because of the optical
phenomenon whereby one looks through narrow railings at the
sea, and they seem to disappear against it, and because the
cemetery railings, symbolic of death, seem abolished by the
contemplation of the divine; 'fausse captive des feuillages'
because it is apparently caught among the leaves. But only
apparently. And the word 'fausse' also points to the sea's
potential liberation from the obsessive situation at the begin-
ning of the poem. 'Secrets éblouissants' is usually taken to be
in apposition to 'captive' and 'golfe': the sea is dazzling, and
its depths mysterious. But it can equally well be in apposition
to 'mes yeux clos': his eyes are secrets because closed; and
'éblouissants' has to do with the dazzling red one sees when
one closes one's eyes against sunlight. Thirdly, the phrase is in
apposition also to 'corps' and 'front', and refers to the secrets of
his future death, 'dazzling' because they are associated with
the dazzling light of eternity. The poet has closed his eyes at
this point because of the introspection he was engaged in
during the last stanza, because of the dazzling light of the
absolute, because of the distress involved in imagining death,
and because at death one's eyes are closed. Death, for the
moment, is seen as a 'dazzling secret'. It is also dazzling
because puzzling to the mind: it involves for example the
paradoxes of 'Quel corps me traîne à sa fin paresseuse,/Quel
front l'attire à cette terre osseuse? [What body drags me to

its lazy end,/What forehead attracts it to this bony earth?]
For the body, though the means of life, does in literal fact
eventually kill its owner; and the mind of the poet is attracted
by the idea of death as the only way of permanently identify-
ing with the absolute, of for ever rejecting change, and by a
Teste-like intellectualism and renunciation of life. 'Traîne'
has an abstract sense of 'draws, leads'; a mental sense of the
body dragging his thoughts down towards death; and concrete
overtones: the dying body *drags*. 'Osseuse' (a nice echo of
'paresseuse') is almost a pun: the earth is 'bony' because hard,
and also because full of bones. An unpleasantly vivid associa-
tion of ideas.

In the next line, 'Une étincelle y pense à mes absents' [A
spark there thinks of my absent ones], 'y' is usually said to refer
to 'front' (forehead). The 'spark' is then an individual idea, in
this case the thought of death. Or else the mind is seen as tiny,
frail, ephemeral, a spark, and Valéry is thinking of his own
mind as just one among millions of human minds. This idea
recalls the eternal fire of which, according to Heraclitus, each
of our souls was a spark. 'Étincelle' also recalls 'scintillation'
(Stanza 4), and 'y' may refer to the sea: a double reference,
which again equates sea with the poet's mind.

Walzer, commenting upon 'mes absents' and 'mes tombeaux'
at the end of the next stanza, notes the tenderness of the
possessive. It is also worth remarking that in so far as this is
the cemetery at Valéry's own birthplace, Sète, these dead
people are literally his own, and that in so far as it is a general-
ized situation, 'any man's death diminishes me'. No sentiment-
ality here: the general identification of the poet with the mass
of human dead is supported by his particular identification
with the dead of Sète. They are 'absent' because no longer
alive, and also because they are unconscious, suffer from
'absence' of mind. (Cf. Stanza 19, where the dead are
referred to as 'têtes inhabitées', empty heads.)

10 Fermé, sacré, plein d'un feu sans matière,
    Fragment terrestre offert à la lumière,
    Ce lieu me plaît, dominé de flambeaux,
    Composé d'or, de pierre et d'arbres sombres,
    Où tant de marbre est tremblant sur tant d'ombres;
    La mer fidèle y dort sur mes tombeaux!

Closed, sacred, full of immaterial fire,
Fragment of earth wide open to the light,
This place appeals, commanded by its torches,
A composition of dark trees, of stone
And gold, with marble tremulous on shadow,
And sleeping on my tombs the faithful sea.

'Fermé': the graveyard is enclosed; also, each grave is closed
up. 'Sacré': this is holy ground, of course. The 'immaterial
fire' ('feu sans matière') is, physically, the sun's light, figurat-
ively, the divine, which is even more immaterial than light.
'Offert à la lumière' [Offered to the light] has a similar double
meaning; and in addition, the dead in cemeteries are in a sense
offered to and awaiting eternity.

The 'flambeaux' are the 'torches du solstice' of Stanza 7,
i.e. the sun's rays. But this time they are also the cypresses:
for 'flambeaux' can mean candlesticks as well as torches; and
'dominer' has the concrete meaning of overlooking as well as the
abstract sense of controlling. The 'gold' in line 4 is principally the
sunlight. The 'trembling' in line 5 is the air shimmering in the
heat so that the tombs appear to do so too. And the 'shadows'
must be taken in a multiple sense: the shadows of tombs and
man in the sunlight, the darkness of the cypress-trees (for
there is a link of sound between 'arbres sombres' and 'ombres')
and the Shades of the dead. The cemetery's brilliant surface
conceals subsurface elements too, dark like the underside of the
mind in Stanzas 7 and 8. The poet's search for perfect light
in the cemetery is doomed to failure.

In the last line, 'La mer fidèle y dort sur mes tombeaux' [The
faithful sea sleeps there upon my tombs], the sea appears *above*
the tombs; and there is a conceit in the use of the word 'fidèle',
which we must link to 'chienne' in the next line: the sea is com-
pared to a faithful sheep-dog. It is 'splendide' because re-
splendent with light, and because magnificent intellectually.

And, since sea is mind, the poet's mind is asleep, at peace, at rest in acceptant contemplation.

But the dog is about to be abruptly wakened:

11 Chienne splendide, écarte l'idolâtre!
Quand solitaire au sourire de pâtre,
Je pais longtemps, moutons mystérieux,
Le blanc troupeau de mes tranquilles tombes,
Éloignes-en les prudentes colombes,
Les songes vains, les anges curieux!

Resplendent watchdog, keep your guard against
The idolater! When I, a solitary,
A smiling shepherd, pasture long my sheep,
The white mysterious flock of peaceful tombs,
Hold off the overprudent doves, the empty
Dreams, the quaint and prying seraphim.

The dog is told to keep out idolaters. Valéry's attitude to 'idolatry' is summed up here: in lines 2–4 he is a shepherd with a flock of mysterious sheep, the tombs (mysterious because concealing their secrets, one of which is death itself). Now this is an echo of the New Testament image of Christ the shepherd of souls. But Valéry is here the shepherd only of the dead, for the emphasis is on the tombs. There is thus an ironic note, an implied denial of survival after death.

The irony continues: the 'doves' are no doubt carved on some of the tombs, and doves are images of the Holy Spirit. We should recall the doves of the opening of the poem. What was, to start with, merely an element in the décor, has here become charged with meaning. And at the end of the poem, in the last line, the doves have disappeared. In short they are not merely metaphors for boats, but stand for a religious attitude which is specifically rejected. At the end of the poem they have vanished. Divine grace has disappeared from the picture. 'Les anges curieux' are both literal angels and those carved on the tombs: they are 'curieux' because quaint, or because prying (like guardian angels). And the 'songes vains' (delusive beliefs in immortality) so resemble 'les anges' in sound that the angels too seem delusory.

The imagery of this stanza brings in certain Christian associa-

tions; and Valéry, who throughout mentions the word God
only in the plural, has (naturally, in a Christian graveyard) at
the back of his mind the ideas of Heaven and the Christian God,
who is, of course, one possible way of viewing the absolute. I
recall asking the way to Valéry's own tomb in the Cemetery of
Sète from an old woman tending the graves there. She told me
I would be disappointed: it was not a 'beautiful tomb' like the
others: it was devoid of decoration; but Madame Valéry had
refused to allow the municipality to erect an ornate monument
for her husband. Naturally! Valéry did not want his tomb to
be covered with sculpted angels and doves, the symbols of a
hope he did not share.

12 Ici venu, l'avenir est paresse.
    L'insecte net gratte la sécheresse;
    Tout est brûlé, défait, reçu dans l'air
    A je ne sais quelle sévère essence . . .
    La vie est vaste, étant ivre d'absence,
    Et l'amertume est douce, et l'esprit clair.

    Once here, the future is pure idleness.
    The brittle insect scrapes at the dry grit.
    All is consumed, destroyed, evaporated
    Into the air, into who knows what stern
    Essence. And life is vast, heady with absence,
    And bitterness is sweet and the mind clear.

Dreams, curiosity and prudence, attributes of the living mind,
which threatened the peace of the tombs in the last stanza,
are inappropriate to the dead. For them, there is no conscious
future, only 'paresse' (idleness): 'Ici venu, l'avenir est paresse':
Buried here, the future is sleep. 'Tout est brûlé, défait, reçu
dans l'air/A je ne sais quelle sévère essence . . .': the
cemetery seems etherealized in the violent meridional sun-
light; there is nothing left at death, or only the 'severest of
essences', which is ambiguously the soul or nothing at all. In
either case, it is essence that survives, not existence. And 'reçu
dans l'air' implies that the soul may even melt into the air,
becoming indistinguishable from it. Aptly, the essence is an
austere one ('sévère'.) As we saw in Stanza 5, the death of the
body is, for Valéry, a disaster for the soul: it becomes smoke

or air: its essence is too rarefied to support reality.

The language in this stanza must, however, be read with its full ambiguity. To some extent it seems to assert the reality of at least some sort of unity with the reigning splendour of the absolute. Life in line 5 is 'vaste'. The poet is seeing life as in some sense enlarged. For if death is seen as the end, but a feared and regretted end, then life is bounded, is a kind of imprison-ment. Here, however, the prison walls have been accepted: consequently they have vanished. 'Ivre d'absence' means both 'greedy for annihilation' and 'intoxicated with non-being'. Intoxication is a state of exaltation. The phrase can be read as an acceptance of Nirvana. In the mystic's total acceptance, opposites are seen as no longer contradictory. Here is one sense of 'l'amertume est douce'. Another is that the bitterness of death, once accepted, ceases to be felt as bitter. Instead, the mind is clear, full of divine light. Or the light may be the pitiless clarity of Teste, rejecting his physical self in favour of the absolute of intellectual purity. Which is a further sense in which the human soul can be blended into the brilliance of the absolute.

But equally, the poet's language is full of implied negatives. The soul is burnt, melted into the air. 'Sécheresse' (dryness) implies aridity. 'Vaste' is also a latinism, meaning 'devastated'. The phrase 'drunk with absence' reminds one of the diminished consciousness of the drunken man: death destroys awareness, one becomes oblivious. The mind in the last line is perhaps so clear that it is empty. And in so far as the lines describe the material situation in the cemetery, they support these inter-pretations. The sun is burning down (line 3); there is an impression of vast emptiness given by 'La vie est vaste, étant ivre d'absence'; there is total stillness but for the cicada scratching away in the dry air.

The reigning brilliance and emptiness of the cemetery stands, then, ambiguously, for a Nirvana-like annihilation or for the aridity of pure intellectual concepts. But the implied negatives of the language suggest that neither of these have any reality. This clarity of intellect or contemplation is so intense that it has become absence of mind.

13 Les morts cachés sont bien dans cette terre
    Qui les réchauffe et sèche leur mystère.
    Midi là-haut, Midi sans mouvement
    En soi se pense et convient à soi-même . . .
    Tête complète et parfait diadème,
    Je suis en toi le secret changement.

The dead lie blanketed and easy here,
Warmed by the earth, their mystery parched away,
While, up above, Noonday the motionless
Suffices to itself and thinks itself . . .
Complete diadem, capital of perfection,
In you I follow, am, the hidden change.

Valéry's attention is now on the substructure of his original metaphor. At the opening of the poem, graveyard, sea, human mind and sky were all bright, calm and stable. On further investigation (Stanzas 7–8) the mind was discovered to contain elements of darkness and instability which were essential to it. It will now be seen to be dark underground too among the dead; the 'reigning splendour' of the outward scene will be negated. But any comparison between the inner man and the state of the dead will also be seen to be impossible, for the dead are still, whereas the living human being is unstable and in motion. Here is the pivot of the poem's metaphoric structure: the 'reigning splendour' of the opening will be rejected as unrealistic: Man's glimpses of the absolute are perforce short, even illusory.

'Les morts cachés sont bien dans cette terre', has two meanings. It is usually taken to be 'The hidden dead are comfortable in this ground', and this fits with the images of dryness and warmth in the next line. But it can also be interpreted as 'they are *in fact* in this ground', which amounts to a denial of survival after death. The effect of such an ambiguity is to make the double assertion it contains more plausible. It reduces our capacity to dissent from either statement, since we cannot accept one without recalling the other.[20] And if they are both comfortable here and in fact here, then the implication is that the warm earth is now their only consolation. This is one reason why their mystery (in line 2) is reduced. And there too we have a case of the support of one set of meanings by another: for both 'réchauffe' and 'sèche' are in literal fact true: the ground warms and dries out the dead bodies.

Now the poet's thoughts turn back to 'Midi là-haut', the agent responsible, in fact, for the warming and drying out of the dead. And the burning presence of the divine, so brightly felt in the first part of this poem, is already somehow a little distanced by the phrase 'là-haut'. The poet states the change-lessness of the absolute: 'Midi sans mouvement'. Here is Aristotle's 'unmoved mover', thinking itself.[21] But a moment later he denies this immobility: 'Je suis en toi le secret change-ment', i.e. 'I follow the secret change in you.' Thus the phrases 'sans mouvement,' 'Tête complète' (complete head) and 'parfait diadème' (perfect diadem), referring in turn to the changelessness of the absolute, to its spiritual or intellectual supremacy and to its completeness, perfection and royalty, are at least in part contradicted. We know that the sun moves; we can follow its movement. And this change is 'secret' because it is impossible to *see* the sun's movement, and because religions do not admit that divinity can change.

There is a further meaning to this last line, that more usually given, namely: 'I *am* the secret change in you', i.e. that Man is the change in the bosom of the absolute. Yes, Man changes, so much is clear. But the observation is to have unfortunate consequences for the divine, as the next stanza shows:

14 Tu n'as que moi pour contenir tes craintes!
Mes repentirs, mes doutes, mes contraintes
Sont le défaut de ton grand diamant . . .
Mais dans leur nuit toute lourde de marbres,
Un peuple vague aux racines des arbres
A pris déjà ton parti lentement.

There is no other to contain your fears!
It is my doubts, repentances, constraints
That are the flaw in your great diamond.
But underneath their stifling night of marble
A shadow folk among the cypress roots
Are on your way already lingering.

Most critics consider that the meaning of 'contenir' in the first
line here is more or less 'experience'. This, taken in conjunc-
tion with the next two lines, makes very good sense. The
divine, apparently changeless and perfect, is contrasted with
Man, who suffers 'repentances', 'doubts' and 'constraints',
which are the mark of a changeable and imperfect being. But
since the divine has created, or at least rules over, imperfection
in the phenomenal world, and since this phenomenal world is
identified with the divine by the perfect mirroring of the
divine's 'great diamond' in it, i.e. by the reflection of sun in
sea, it has created imperfection in itself. By poetically equating
the absolute, the sun, the sea, mind and life, Valéry has,
within the context of his poem, suggested imperfection in the
absolute. The diamond (the sun, and the divine crown of
royalty) is flawed.

'Mais . . .' marks a fall from the exaltation of the last few
lines, and their proud assertion of the importance of Man. For
the second implication of these first three lines was: How can
Man, fearful, repentant, doubting, constrained, achieve a
perfection like that of the absolute? The answer given is,
Only in death: it is the dead alone who, in line 6, have 'sided
with the divine'. Yes, but what irony, if only in death can Man
be perfect. The absolute and negation are almost equated. The
concreteness of this description of the dead needs no under-
lining: they are 'dans leur nuit', the darkness of the tomb, the
eternal night of death, the darkness below the ground. 'Une
nuit lourde' is an oppressive night; but also there is the weight
of the tombstones lying on the dead. 'Un peuple vague'
suggests they are dim, shadowy, indeterminate, ghostly; the
adjective doubts their existence. The adverb 'lentement'
reminds one of the slow decomposition of the dead; and
perhaps also means so slow that everything has stopped for
them, for there is a contrast between the tense and the adverb,
and the tense implies finality.

As for the force of 'déjà': for the dead it is now too late, but
for the spectator there is still time.

15 Ils ont fondu dans une absence épaisse,
   L'argile rouge a bu la blanche espèce,
   Le don de vivre a passé dans les fleurs !
   Où sont des morts les phrases familières,
   L'art personnel, les âmes singulières ?
   La larve file où se formaient des pleurs.

They have dissolved into a dense absence,
Their human whiteness drunk by the red clay,
The gift of life has passed on to the flowers.
Where are the dead's familiar turns of speech,
Personal talents, individual souls ?
The larva threads where tears used to form.

The picture becomes darker: 'They have melted' (both
physically and figuratively) 'into thick absence'. This absence
is made like a presence by the concreteness of the adjective
'thick'. Also the word strengthens 'absence', and implies
'complete absence'. Also the word refers to the dense earth
they have become, as in line 2. 'L'argile rouge a bu la blanche
espèce' [The red clay has drunk the white species]: 'drunk' is
appropriate where the dead have 'melted'; and it suggests the
idea of reabsorption. The clay is red and the flesh white not
only because of their actual colour, no doubt. For what is 'la
blanche espèce' ? Not only the white race, but also the dead,
white with the pallor of death. With their whiteness is con-
trasted the red clay, colour of blood, because it seems alive by
contrast with the dead. It is perhaps almost 'blooodthirsty'.
And redness is dimly associated through blood with guilt. 'Le
don de vivre a passé dans les fleurs' [The gift of life has passed
on to the flowers] gives us again the idea of reabsorption: it
is a cliché, but literal fact, that new life feeds upon the dead:
the torch of life is passed from hand to hand. To put the ques-
tion in the next line, 'Où sont des morts les phrases fami-
lières . . . ?' [Where are the familiar phrases of the dead . . . ?]
implies that the dead are in fact nowhere. Each man was single,
unique, separate, special—but also strange and remarkable—
for so individuals are. And Valéry thinks of himself, and of
artists like him: 'Où (est) . . . l'art personnel . . . ?' [Where
(is their) personal art . . . ?]
   The answer to this question is, indeed, Worse than nowhere.

For, 'La larve file où se formaient des pleurs' [The larva threads where tears used to form]. This is vividly unpleasant. 'Filer' means principally to spin, but also to flow (like a liquid), to slip by (like time), to move on. And where is 'où se formaient des pleurs'? In the mind, in the brain, in the eyes. It is not tears *for* the dead that are mentioned here. For to what purpose? But tears of the dead in time gone by. A subtlety which avoids sentimentality and achieves emotion. 'Larve', by the way, does not only mean 'larva, worm or grub'; it also reminds one of the Latin 'larva', which was the ghost of a man who had died in tragic circumstances.

16 Les cris aigus des filles chatouillées,
   Les yeux, les dents, les paupières mouillées,
   Le sein charmant qui joue avec le feu,
   Le sang qui brille aux lèvres qui se rendent,
   Les derniers dons, les doigts qui les défendent,
   Tout va sous terre et rentre dans le jeu!

The shrill cries of girls teased and tickled,
The shining eyes and teeth, the moist eyelids,
The charming breast playing with fire, the blood
Glowing at their surrendering lips, the last
Favours, the hands defending them, it all
Goes under earth and back into the game.

For the moment, an abrupt reversal of atmosphere: five lines of the utmost sensuousness. There are few ambiguities here that require noting, but 'chatouillées' is both literal and metaphorical (teased by desire); 'joue avec le feu' is not merely the old cliché of playing with fire, but also refers to a particular fire, that of love; and 'le sang qui brille aux lèvres qui se rendent' [the blood shining at surrendering lips] does not only mean what it literally appears to do, but also has a less polite sense, assisted by the euphemism 'les derniers dons' [the last gifts].

Death reappears in the last line, following immediately upon the imagery of life and love, so that it appears darker, and they brighter, by contrast. Indeed, could this stanza not also be interpreted as the rape of beauty by death? Interpreting it thus, the word 'derniers' is aptly used: on the face of things it implies the ultimate sexual gift; but secondarily, it can suggest the last gift of all, the surrender of life to death. Reabsorption is implied again in 'Tout . . . rentre dans le jeu' [Everything . . . goes back again into the game]. The game referred to is the round-dance of Nature, flesh to earth, earth to plants, plants to food, food to flesh. But also we are given the idea that nothing is serious, that life is a game, that the gods are playing with us.

17 Et vous, grande âme, espérez-vous un songe
    Qui n'aura plus ces couleurs de mensonge
    Qu'aux yeux de chair l'onde et l'or font ici ?
    Chanterez-vous quand serez vaporeuse ?
    Allez ! Tout fuit ! Ma présence est poreuse,
    La sainte impatience meurt aussi !

And you, fine soul, are you in hopes to see
A dream without the illusive colouring
This gold and water have for mortal eyes ?
Tell me : when thou art vapour, wilt thou sing ?
Come, come ! The world is fugitive, my presence
Porous, even divine impatience dies !

So much, then, for the survival of the body. Valéry turns to address his soul, and to deny the permanence and divinity that it seemed to have in the early part of the poem. 'Grande âme' has a touch of irony about it. And the whole stanza has an ironic note: the poet is achieving sufficient detachment to reject this horrifying vision of mortality, as also to reject any possible consolation. We can paraphrase the first three lines as 'Do you hope for a reality behind the transitory, for immortality after death ?' 'Songe' means 'dream', which suggests that such hopes are illusory, and refers back to and adds to the earlier use of 'songe' in Stanza 2 and 'sommeil' in Stanza 3. The dream which was knowledge in Stanza 2 has now an overtone of doubt attached to it; and the 'sleep' which lay beneath the sea's shining surface is linked with the death which was, as we saw in Stanza 8, at the back of the human mind. The illusory nature of such dreams is underlined by the rime with 'mensonge' (lie). The word is also appropriate in the context of a supposed arousal from the 'sleep' of death: 'But in that sleep what dreams may come ?' as Shakespeare has it. 'Espérer' means 'to hope for': but in Languedocien, the still surviving language of Valéry's part of France, it means 'to await': so we have here another double sense. 'L'onde et l'or' describes the fancy glitter of sunlight on the waves, that is of the divine in the human mind. This image of the divine now appears delusory. The idea is the more convincing because one remembers that the glitter is only a surface glitter: the depths of the sea remain dark.

'Chanterez-vous quand serez vaporeuse?' [Will you sing when (you) are vaporous?] Impossible, for what would you sing with? 'Vaporeuse' is beautiful, particularly in its echo of 'poreuse' in the next line; and it picks up the imagery attached to ghosts right through the poem, the 'smoke' in Stanza 5, the 'shadow' in Stanza 6, the soul 'reçu dans l'air/A je ne sais quelle sévère essence' in Stanza 12, the 'vague'ness of the dead in Stanza 14. The personal pronoun is dropped in front of 'serez', giving us the flavour of medieval poetry, of Villon or of paintings of the Dance of Death, or the atmosphere of the Epicurean type of poetry, or 'style marotique'.

An abrupt change of tone at 'Allez!'—an ironic appeal to commonsense: 'Come, come! You and I know things aren't like that!' For 'Tout fuit'. This is the equivalent of πάντα ῥεῖ, Plato's gloss on Heraclitus; and a commonplace in European thought about time. 'Ma présence est poreuse' implies that the soul can slip through the body like water through earthenware. And porosity has overtones of unsolidity and of the ephemeral, an impression heightened by its echo of 'vaporeuse'. 'La sainte impatience' is 'sainte' because it is impatience *for* immortality; because impatience is valuable; and because it is a synonym for the 'worm of life', the 'life-force' that we encounter two stanzas further on.

18 Maigre immortalité noire et dorée,
    Consolatrice affreusement laurée,
    Qui de la mort fais un sein maternel,
    Le beau mensonge et la pieuse ruse!
    Qui ne connaît, et qui ne les refuse,
    Ce crâne vide et ce rire éternel!

18 Gaunt immortality in black and gold,
   Consoler grimly wreathed in laurel, making
   Believe that death's a warm maternal breast,
   Sublime falsehood, consecrated fraud!
   Who does not recognize them and reject
   That empty skull, that everlasting grin!

Immortality is 'meagre' in the first line because it has little to
offer: a tomb, say, and a bit of carving; it is also *thin* in an
almost literal sense: for one thinks of the gauntness of the
human skeleton. The whole stanza in fact presents us with
images of immortality which suggest, not immortality, but
annihilation. The pleasant clashes more and more painfully
with the unpleasant, as the stanza progresses. Pleasant are
'immortalité, dorée, consolatrice, laurée, sein maternel, beau,
pieuse, rire'; unpleasant are 'maigre, noire, affreusement,
mensonge, ruse, crâne vide', and again 'rire'. Thus, a terrible
irony is spread over the promise of immortality. 'Affreusement'
cancels 'laurée' and 'consolatrice'. This laurel-wreath may be
specifically the poet's immortality, in the sense of his posthum-
ous fame; this too is rejected as but cold comfort. Efforts to
insist on the reality of life after death are recognized in line 4
as *really* beautiful and pious, but also as ironically so. For
instance the Church's painted pictures of eternal life are
beautiful, but these pictures are lies. 'Beau mensonge' repeats
the idea of gilding the dark that we have in line 1: the evil of
death has been given a surface sheen of goodness.

Valéry appeals to personal experience again, as he had with
'Allez! Tout fuit!' in the last stanza. 'Qui ne connaît, et qui ne
les refuse,/Ce crâne vide et ce rire éternel!' [Who does not
know, and who does not refuse them,/This empty skull and this
everlasting laughter!] No one in solemn fact can reconcile
himself to the idea of his own death. To support this there is an
appeal to the almost material horror which the dead inspire:
'Ce crâne vide': literally the empty skull, metaphorically the
dead man's loss of awareness; 'et ce rire éternel', which is an
ironic image of great compactness. For laughter can signify
joy, hence 'eternal joy'. But one thinks at the same time of the
grinning skull. What sort of laughter is this, in fact? Madness?
Mockery? (The skeleton might be laughing at us because we
shall one day resemble him.) Superimposed on the consolatory

sense of laughter, these ghastly associations undermine it. Or
is it, again, the laughter of the gods as they play with us?
(Cf. the last line of Stanza 16.) In this final word the clashing
opposites, the pleasant and unpleasant associations of death,
which had hitherto been expressed by pairs of mutually
contrasting words, at last meet, and cancel each other. We are
left with nothing, with the image of the grinning skull.

19 Pères profonds, têtes inhabitées,
    Qui sous le poids de tant de pelletées,
    Etes la terre et confondez nos pas,
    Le vrai rongeur, le ver irréfutable
    N'est point pour vous qui dormez sous la table,
    Il vit de vie, il ne me quitte pas!

    Profound forefathers, empty-headed ghosts,
    Who under the weight of so much shovelled earth
    Are mingled with it and confound our steps,
    The real, the irrefutable gnawing worm
    Is not for you, asleep beneath the table,
    He lives on life, he never gives me rest!

'Pères profonds' echoes Virgil's phrase 'manesque profundi'.[22]
The French and Latin senses are 'ancestors deep down'; a
further French sense is 'profound with the wisdom of death'.
But this is ironic, for it is immediately followed by the phrase
'têtes inhabitées' (which echoes 'crâne vide', and which is a
reminiscence of Homer's phrase 'νεκύων ἀμενηνὰ κάρηνα').[23]
The dead 'are' the earth; they cannot distinguish our steps,
either from each other, or from the earth itself. Or they
'confound' our steps as in the Biblical English sense: i.e. they
make one doubt the reality of our own living movement. This
sense of the phrase foreshadows Stanza 21 and the philo-
sophical problem of movement and immobility. On the whole,
however, in this stanza, we have an assertion of the unreality
of the dead. Thus, in line 5, the 'table' is not only an image for
the tombstone; it is also the table at which the dead held the
feast of life; and now they lie in a drunken stupor under it.

The suggestion we have been given that the dead are really
dead, unconscious, snuffed out, will now be contrasted with
the consciousness of the living. The Biblical 'worm that dieth

not' is evoked, with its associations: (1) the torments of Hell, since the phrase was traditionally explained as description of these torments by Jesus;[24] (2) our disgust at the spectacle of a decaying corpse, due to our habit of identifying ourselves with our fellow-humans. Hence an irrational fear that the dead man may feel the worms. The 'worm of the living' is contrasted with this: their worm is a symbol for sensation and consciousness. The worm of the dead is not a 'true' worm, for it cannot be felt. 'Le vrai rongeur, le ver irréfutable' lives only in a living creature ('Il vit de vie', sense 1). It is 'rongeur' because it can be an image for life itself, which in a sense feeds upon the living creature, eats him away, ages him, and eventually kills him ('Il vit de vie', sense 2). This identification of life with the worm is supported by alliteration: 'Vrai, ver, vous, vit, vie', as it will be again in the next stanza: 'Voit, veut, vivant, vie'. Finally, Valéry's personal obsession with investigating his own consciousness is intended. For 'ver rongeur' is a French cliché, usually meaning the 'pangs of remorse', but capable of standing for any obsessive preoccupation. If one recalls the poet's statement about 'une théorie de la Connaissance',[25] one can see that the image of the 'ver rongeur' very neatly fits the idea of consciousness looking at itself, analysing itself fragment by fragment: 'Le Serpent se mange la queue.' ('Worm' is not too distant, poetically, from 'serpent'!) 'Mais, ce n'est qu'après un long temps de mastication qu'il reconnaît le goût du serpent. Il s'arrête alors. Mais, au bout d'un autre temps, n'ayant rien d'autre à manger, il s'y remet. Il arrive alors à avoir sa tête dans sa gueule. C'est ce qu'il appelle: "une théorie de la Connaissance". '[The Serpent eats his own tail. But it is only after a long period of mastication that he recognizes the taste of serpent. So he stops. But, after further time has elapsed, since he has nothing else to eat, he begins again. He ends up with his head in his gullet. This is what he calls a theory of Knowledge.] One may appropriately look forward to the image 'Sa dent secrète est de moi si prochaine' [His secret tooth is so close to me . . .] in the next stanza. The idea is very similar. And since self-investigation is *reflexive*, resembles the action of gazing into a mirror, it is apt enough that Valéry should twice give us phrases with a reflexive effect: 'Il vit de vie . . .', and, in the next stanza, 'A ce vivant je vis d'appartenir!'

20 Amour, peut-être, ou de moi-même haine ?
    Sa dent secrète est de moi si prochaine
    Que tous les noms lui peuvent convenir !
    Qu'importe ! Il voit, il veut, il songe, il touche !
    Ma chair lui plaît, et jusque sur ma couche,
    A ce vivant je vis d'appartenir !

Self-love, maybe, or hatred of myself?
His secret hunger biting in so close
That any name would suit him equally.
No matter! For he sees, wills, thinks and touches,
I am his meat and even on my couch
I live through my belonging to his life.

It will now be clear why Valéry asks 'Amour, peut-être, ou de moi-même haine ?' For obsession with one's own awareness is a sort of self-love. But the self-analysis involved is a sort of self-destruction, and entails considerable mental discomfort and a pitiless detachment. He then goes on to state that self-investigation 'est de moi si prochaine/Que tous les noms lui peuvent convenir !' [is so close to me/That all names can suit it]. Even names which contradict each other? we ask. It would seem so: hate and love represent our basic creative and destructive instincts. So we can add to our view of the 'worm', that it is not merely an intellectual restlessness, but is associated at the deepest levels of the mind with our emotions. The meaning here would seem to be, approximately, that at the very heart of consciousness, in the refined self-torment of the intellect itself, the most basic human emotions are still present. But 'tous les noms' is not only all-inclusive: it is so inclusive as to be completely vague. These deep regions of the self-regarding mind are so rarefied that they become incapable of definition: one is reminded of Valéry's Monsieur Teste, whose attainment of purity of thought, purity of self-inspection, resulted, we are told, in a sort of negation of his personality: he seemed characterless, 'quelconque'. Another reason why self-investigation is, perhaps, 'hatred of oneself'. Moreover, not only does the result entail destruction of one's inessential features (such as personality); it would also entail, in a hypothetical state of absolute knowledge of ourselves, an abandonment of all action. Teste says: 'Si nous savions, nous ne parlerions pas—nous ne penserions pas, nous ne nous parlerions pas.' [If we knew, we wouldn't speak—we wouldn't think, we wouldn't talk to ourselves.][26]

The reader may, by this time, be thoroughly puzzled. For we have identified the 'worm' not only with life, but also with that extreme state of self-consciousness, of self-cannibalism almost, in which all non-contemplative action is impossible. The latter is precisely the view of Lawler: the 'worm', he says, is abstract thought, and this renders movement impossible. In previous stanzas death had been the threat to the body, and abstract thought is now seen as the threat to the mind. This leads neatly on to the next stanza, in which Zeno's paradoxes represent the final temptation of the absolute towards immobility. I think Lawler is mistaken, however, in taking the 'worm' as symbolic of one idea *only*, namely abstract thought. And, in so far as the 'worm' *does* stand for abstract thought, it would seem to be physical movement that is in danger of being reduced to immobility: it is, in short, life that is being threatened, rather than the mind.

But how can the same symbol be used for both life and inaction? The answer is that what might make nonsense rationally is often good logic poetically. The consciousness regards itself; enjoys doing so ('A ce vivant je vis d'appartenir' [I live through my belonging to this living being] in the sense of 'take delight in'); is only aware of its own life when regarding itself ('A ce vivant je vis', in the sense of 'feel alive'). The 'worm' is Valéry's 'cogito ergo sum': the fact that the consciousness can regard itself is the only proof of life to oneself (a further sense of 'a ce vivant je vis d'appartenir'). But this vital essence can also tend in the opposite direction: it can be centrifugal as well as centripetal: it can see outside itself, will, and initiate action ('Il voit, il veut . . . il touche'). The 'worm' in short symbolizes the problem of being and knowing, a problem which can perhaps be most clearly stated like this: How can one *know* one's existence except when contemplating oneself? But how can one *exist* except in action, i.e. when one is not contemplating oneself?

It is right that at this stage of the poem action and inaction should be confronted. For Zeno's paradoxes are about to be called upon as concrete illustrations of the opposition: and the one is about to be rejected in favour of the other. And if there still appears to be a paradox, well, so there seems to have been for the poet himself. For, as he says of the Zeno stanza, 'J'ai débauché les quelques images de Zénon à exprimer la rébellion contre la durée et l'acuité d'une méditation qui fait sentir trop cruellement l'écart entre l'*être* et le *connaître* que développe la conscience de la conscience.' [I misapplied Zeno's few images in expressing a rebellion against the duration and stringency of a meditation which makes one perceive all too cruelly that gulf between *being* and *knowing* which is developed by consciousness of consciousness.][27] The gap is about to be bridged by a spark: action is about to succeed contemplation. Certainly the nature of the spark will remain mysterious: it is like whatever it is that comes 'entre le vide et l'événement pur'; it is like the mysterious 'Will' which bridges the gap between thought and action; it is what Valéry calls 'la puissance réflexe actuelle, dont le sursaut brise et dissipe un état de fixité sombre . . .' [the immediate reflex force, whose impulse breaks and dissipates a state of dark fixity.][28] Neither Valéry's terminology nor the word 'Will' explains anything: one might as well write a question-mark. But, as the next stanza will illustrate, we know as a matter of experience that, somehow, the current passes, motion does occur.

21 Zénon! Cruel Zénon! Zénon d'Élée!
    M'as-tu percé de cette flèche ailée
    Qui vibre, vole, et qui ne vole pas!
    Le son m'enfante et la flèche me tue!
    Ah! le soleil . . . Quelle ombre de tortue
    Pour l'âme, Achille immobile à grands pas!

    Zeno! Cruel Zeno! Zeno of Elea!
    And have you pinned me down with your barbed arrow
    Vibrating, flying and which cannot fly!
    The sound engenders me, the arrow kills!
    Ah! the sun . . . For the soul a tortoise-shadow,
    Achilles at full stride and motionless!

Valéry's remark that this stanza was only inserted to lend a little philosophical colour to the poem, has been much quoted. But to quote him thus is to misquote him. In fact, the poet's words are: 'Mais je n'ai entendu prendre à la philosophie qu'un peu de sa *couleur*.' [But all I intended to take from philosophy was a little of its *colour*.]29 This does *not* mean that the purpose of inserting this stanza (which was, indeed, one of the first Valéry wrote in his original sketches of the poem) was to give philosophical colour; but that the stanza itself is not philosophical but merely has the atmosphere of philosophy, is not an intellectual statement but an emotional one, is not, in short, prose but poetry.

That this is a way of feeling rather than a way of thinking, is evident in the repetition of the appeal to Zeno: 'Zénon! Cruel Zénon! Zénon d'Élée!' Exclamations are indices of emotion—repeated exclamations more so. But to appreciate even the emotion in this stanza, we have to resort to the intellect. Zeno of Elea, a fifth-century philosopher, a follower of Parmenides, is supposed to have held, with his master, that 'What *is*, is a finite, spherical, motionless corporeal *plenum*, and there is nothing beyond it. The appearance of multiplicity and motion, empty space and time, are illusions.'30 In attacking the opposite point of view that 'What is' was a multiplicity, he resorted to a number of paradoxes, of which those that have survived are still famous, entertaining and puzzling. His argument about the arrow (line 2) goes as follows: at each moment of its path through the air, the arrow corresponds exactly with a motionless line upon its trajectory; but if it corresponds exactly, how can it move?

'Le son' in line 4 may refer either to the sound of the arrow (which 'vibrates' in line 8) or to another argument of Zeno's, that of the millet-seed. One grain, dropped, makes no sound; but a thousand grains do: $1,000 \times 0 = 1,000$. 'Son' is thus a pun, meaning both 'bran' and 'the sound of the bran'. What relevance has this to the argument? It can be taken to imply the reverse of the Achilles paradox, which we will discuss in a moment, and in which space is chopped into progressively smaller and smaller lengths, and motion is denied. In the case of the millet-seed, sound appears to be asserted as real despite the soundlessness of its units. In one case, subdivision is used to deny Reality, in the other, multiplication is used to assert Reality. Un-Eleatic though this may seem, Valéry seems to be using the image this way. For there is an opposition implied between 'Le son m'enfante' (the sound gives me life, makes me see life is real) and 'la flèche me tue'.

The paradox of Achilles and the tortoise is better known: Achilles travels, say, twice as fast as the tortoise. The tortoise is ten yards ahead of him. Achilles travels those ten yards. But the tortoise has by then travelled another five. Achilles travels those five. But the tortoise has then travelled 2·5. Achilles travels those 2·5. But the tortoise has then travelled 1·25. And so on. Achilles never overtakes the tortoise! Thus, the reality of motion appears to be disproved.

But the image of Achilles and the tortoise is not merely spatial. In the context of the self-regarding consciousness, it has a mental application too. For the process of dividing space up into ever smaller and smaller lengths is similar to that of the consciousness looking at itself, then looking at itself looking at itself, and so on, fining itself away, 're' fining itself. And the contemplation of both has a similar effect: in one case one begins to think action is impossible; in the other one has the apparent cessation of action. As Valéry himself says, 'L'*âme* naïvement veut épuiser l'infini de l'Eléate.' [The *soul* wishes, naïvely, to exhaust the Eleatic's infinite.] [31] Since Zeno is supposed, like Parmenides, to have believed in a finite universe, I take this statement to refer to the infinite regression involved both in consciousness of consciousness and in Zeno's paradoxes.

Where is the flaw in Zeno's argument? According to more than one authority, he has not yet been finally answered. To do so is a philosopher's task, not mine. Besides it is possible that Zeno did not so much wish to demonstrate the impossibility of motion as to demolish the arguments of his opponents by showing them that motion was as difficult to account for in their system as in his own. [32] On this account of his intentions, it is clear that his paradoxes are double-edged; for there is no absurdity attached to them *unless we are committed to believing that movement is real after all*. And that it is real, is underlined by Valéry. For the sound of the arrow in the air (lines 3 and 4) proves its movement (here is another meaning of the words 'le son m'enfante'); and the fact that it can kill us proves that we were alive.

But the arrow is not only the arrow in Zeno's story. It is also a metaphor for the story itself, or the point(!) Zeno is making. [33] In this sense, the arrow (the story) could 'kill' Valéry, since all his attempts to act would be futile: life itself would be

meaningless. There is a further sense too: for, despite the ex-
clamation mark,[34] the words 'M'as-tu percé' have an inter-
rogative form. We can roughly paraphrase this sense as
follows: 'Have you killed me with your arrow (i.e. the real
arrow in the story)? According to you, Zeno, you cannot—for
movement is unreal. But if you cannot, then I am not con-
vinced by your story of the arrow: for your arrow (i.e. the point
of the story) cannot, according to you, kill me (i.e. convince
me).' This is a sophistic argument to say the least! But witty
and poetic, and I am not sure it is any more fallacious than
Zeno's own. The philosopher is, so to speak, refuted out of his
own mouth and by his own methods.

At this point we are reminded of the sun: 'Ah! le soleil . . .',
symbol of immobility, so that in one sense, the appeal to the sun
registers agreement with Zeno. But if the 'ombre de tortue'
(tortoise shadow) refers to the sun, the interpretation is
different: it may move invisibly slowly, but move it does. Or,
if we take the sun as motionless even here, then the contrast
is between moving Achilles and unmoving sun: 'We', Valéry
is saying, 'are not like the absolute, changeless.' Again, if
'ombre de tortue' is in apposition to Achilles, then he is
apparently motionless. And there is a tone of impatience in the
exclamation 'Quelle ombre de tortue . . .!', an impatience
which will resolve itself in action in the next stanza. Again,
Achilles could be in apposition to 'âme', so that the human soul
is likened to Achilles seeming to move, but in eternity, motion-
less. And then we have irony, a clash between the tortoise
image of Achilles and the Achilles image of the soul: the soul
appears stable and constant to us, but we know it is in fact
moving on, changing, approaching death. 'Immobile à grands
pas' is itself ironic too: we are meant to reject the notion of
immobility and admit that Achilles does move. And indeed
the notion of large units of measurement, present in 'à grands
pas', is perhaps fatal to the paradox: why, if Zeno describes
Achilles as travelling ten yards in the first instance, can he not
admit he does so again? Measurement itself entails movement.

Finally, we have here Valéry's personal concern with
introspection, linked with his awareness that too much of it is
fatal to the creator. He points out that, if we had to think of
all the processes involved in taking each single step, we
should not be able to walk at all: 'Il est à croire que notre acte

le plus simple, notre geste le plus familier, ne pourrait s'accomplir, et que la moindre de nos pouvoirs nous serait obstacle, si nous devions nous le rendre présent à l'esprit et le connaître à fond pour l'exercer.' [It is to be supposed that our simplest action, our most ordinary gesture, could not be accomplished, and that our most trivial faculty would be an obstacle to us, if we could not exercise it without being conscious of and completely conversant with it.][35] This is entirely true: no one can be recommended to consider his physical actions as he is walking downstairs: he would be certain to trip over himself! Valéry continues: 'Achille ne peut vaincre la tortue s'il songe à l'espace et au temps.' [Achilles cannot beat the tortoise if he thinks of space and time.][36] The poet cannot conquer his poem if he thinks too much about the processes involved in creation; the man cannot act if he thinks too much about the processes involved in action. And here we should perhaps, with Lawler, underline 'Pour l'âme': it is only to the *soul* that the arguments of Zeno make sense: the *body* knows them to be nonsense.

Now because Zeno was attempting to prove that the phenomenal world, the world of space and time, is unreal, and that 'What is' is motionless and eternal (in the sense of being outside time), an opinion which seemed to be precisely that of the poet at the beginning of *le Cimetière marin*—because too of the poet's reminder of this state of affairs, in his exclamation 'Ah! le soleil . . .!'—we have now been given the link between action and inaction on the one hand, and the divine and the phenomenal world on the other. The reality of 'inaction' and of the divine has, in the context of the poem, been 'disproved'; the reality of 'action' and of the phenomenal world has been 'demonstrated'.

The argument, or rather the contrasting attitudes, expressed in the stanza, seem extraordinarily complex and rarefied. Would Valéry himself have approved of this attempt to explain them? He himself says of this stanza:

'(ces vers) déterminent . . . plus précisément *la personne qui parle*—un amateur d'abstractions' (i.e. they represent Valéry's own concern with the problems of pure thought, action appearing out of inaction, etc.) '. . . ils opposent enfin à ce qui fut de spéculatif et de trop attentif en lui la puissance réflexe actuelle, dont le sursaut brise et dissipe un état de fixité sombre, et comme complémentaire de la splendeur régnante' (i.e. this is where the problems of action and of inaction meet, and action comes out the victor) 'en même temps qu'elle' (la puissance réflexe actuelle) 'bouleverse un ensemble de *jugements* sur toutes choses humaines, inhumaines et surhumaines' [These lines define more precisely *the person speaking*—a lover of abstractions . . . and finally they confront everything that had been speculative and over-attentive in him, with the immediate reflex force, whose impulse breaks and dissipates a state of dark fixity which had been so to speak complementary to the reigning splendour; at the same time as it (the immediate reflex force) 'overthrows a set of *judgments* on everything human, inhuman and superhuman'],[37] (i.e. the metaphysical attitudes of the opening of the poem are now left behind, dropped as no longer relevant: we have discarded contemplation; we now discard metaphysical speculation altogether).

22 Non, non! . . . Debout! Dans l'ère successive!
Brisez, mon corps, cette forme pensive!
Buvez, mon sein, la naissance du vent!
Une fraîcheur, de la mer exhalée,
Me rend mon âme . . . O puissance salée!
Courons à l'onde en rejaillir vivant!

No, no! . . . Stand up! Into successive time!
Breathe, my lungs, the birth of the wind! Shatter,
My body, this reflective attitude!
A freshness, exhalation of the sea,
Restores to me my soul . . . Salt potency!
Let's run to the waves and be flung back alive!

'Non, non!' A double rejection of Zeno's outlook—for the temptation was strong. 'Dans l'ère successive!' An assertion of the reality of movement through time, that is to say, through our own mode of time, where moment succeeds moment: a contrast is implied with eternity, the mode of time where succession does not exist. It is also an acceptance of this movement; an impatience to be up and act, which follows from the impatience expressed in the previous stanza by

'Quelle ombre de tortue . . .!' It is the body that rescues the poet from fixity and darkness: 'Brisez, mon corps, cette forme pensive!' The 'forme pensive' is the attitude of the body in repose and thought; also, thought itself; also the particular form the thoughts took. The poet becomes aware of his body, feels himself breathing. The wind rises over the sea. And this is a kind of rebirth for him; it is like the child, reborn, taking its first breath. The sea, the ultimate origin of life, is appropriately associated with this idea: the salt content of our blood is still approximately that of the sea, and 'O puissance salée' apostrophizes the sea, the blood, the bitter-sweet experience of life itself. There is a connexion with the word '*exhalée*' here, for this appears to contain the Greek root for 'salt' (ἅλς). Out of inaction, action; after indulgence in pure thought, a reminder of the rights and demands of the body. As for the cemetery, it is no longer noticed in these last stanzas: both death and death-like immobility have been rejected.

'Une fraîcheur me rend mon âme': Clearly this soul is not a soul in the religious sense: it is synonymous with movement, with life. The phrase 'me rend mon âme' is not rhetoric: for 'âme' is from the Latin 'anima' which meant both 'soul' and 'breath': the animating principle, in short. A further interpretation of the phrase is that, unlike in 'cogito ergo sum', it is not here consciousness of consciousness that is proving life, but the 'freshness exhaled from the sea': the soul, i.e. the awareness of life, is given back to the poet through his senses. And in the last line of the stanza, the mind accepts the activity of the body, and the immersion of the senses in the sea of life. Elsewhere, Valéry writes apropos of swimming: 'Il me semble que je me retrouve et me reconnaisse quand je reviens à cette eau universelle.' [It seems to me that I rediscover and recognize myself when I return to this universal water.][38]

23 Oui! Grande mer de délires douée,
    Peau de panthère et chlamyde trouée
    De mille et mille idoles du soleil,
    Hydre absolue, ivre de ta chair bleue,
    Qui te remords l'étincelante queue
    Dans un tumulte au silence pareil,

23 Yes! Immense sea, dowered with ecstasy,
Rippling skin of panther, ruffled chlamys
Holed with a myriad idols of the sun,
Intoxicated with your own blue flesh,
O Hydra free and absolute, who bite
Your sparkling tail in tumult like a silence,

As the last stanza opened with 'Non!' so this one opens with
'Oui!' The mind accepts the body, action, movement and
restlessness; for the aspect the sea now presents, under the
influence of the wind, is rough and turbulent: it is a 'grande
mer de délires douée'. The 'délires' are, materially, its storms,
its inner mysteries; figuratively, the activity of the body. But
'sea' was also, in the early part of the poem, 'mind'; and it
remains mind here too, though this is no longer the mind in
contemplation, but the mind in action, full of 'deliriums',
imagination, inspiration, turbulence.

'Peau de panthère' is partly a visual image for the many-
coloured sea, dappled with waves, troughs of waves and
shifting colours, smooth as a feline pelt. It also refers to the
sometimes ferocious contents of the mind. And the Greek
origin of the word ($\pi\acute{a}\nu\theta\eta\rho$) was at one time supposed to be
$\pi\hat{a}\nu$ and $\theta\acute{\eta}\rho$, i.e. all-beast: which links with the many-headed
hydra two lines further on. The panther was sacred to Diony-
sos, the nature god of wine and ecstatic emotion, who was
sometimes represented wearing a panther-skin or riding on a
panther; and we might call the emotion in these lines almost
Dionysiac. A 'chlamys' is an ancient Greek garment, whose
folds may remind one of the waves. It was often colourful, and
it was the dress of hunters, travellers, soldiers and youths, in
short, of the active man. No doubt it belongs here to Achilles,
symbol of action in Stanza 21. It is 'trouée/De mille et mille
idoles du soleil' [Holed/with a thousand thousand idols of the
sun], because its myriad waves bear each a reflection of the
sun. But this is to take 'idoles' as being simply the transcription
of the Greek $\epsilon\acute{i}\delta\omega\lambda o\nu$, an 'image'. Even in Greek, however,
it also meant an 'idol'; and recalling that the sun symbolized
the divine, it is clear that the usual sense of 'idol' (a false
image) is meant here as well as the sense 'image'. The mind is
'holed' (pierced, permeated) by the ideas of the divine, or of
a multiplicity of gods, that it contains. 'Hydre' is a pun on the

Greek stem ὕδρ—(water). The hydra was a many-headed monster, as the sea is a many-waved monster, has countless monsters within it, and is a metaphor for life, i.e. is 'many-headed' in that it contains the totality of living creatures in it, is in short an 'all-beast'. Why is it 'absolute'? Because the sea is life (which is all there is, hence the nearest we can get to an absolute); because it is the human mind (which is self-sufficient, and which contains notions of the absolute); and because one of the Latin senses of the word was 'liberated' (absolutus). The present liberated state of the sea contrasts with its calm captivity in Stanza 9—though this was only an apparent captivity [the sea there was a 'fausse captive'.)—where it was trapped by sun and cemetery and by all they stand for. Finally, it also means 'come to completion': the sea is completed in that it has brought forth the 'many heads' of life, and that it is now fully itself again, liberated from the 'reigning splendour'.

It is not to be supposed however that consciousness of consciousness, that self-investigation, has been utterly rejected: it has its place here. For the 'hydra' is 'ivre de sa chair bleue' and '(se) remord l'étincelante queue'. Which reminds us of the 'worm' eating away at the poet's mind, and of the serpent eating its own tail (hydras are also watersnakes). Self-investigation is still in order. But there is an additional meaning. 'Chair' recalls the physical and organic aspects of Man; the mind desires, needs and depends upon the body, is greedy *for* and drunk *with* the body. 'Ivre de sa chair bleue' is the diametric opposite of 'ivre d'absence' (Stanza 12).

'Dans un tumulte au silence pareil': the noise of the waves has now become so constant as to be as steady as silence. Also, the phrase recalls the state of tranquillity at the start of the poem, and reminds us that that tranquillity was only apparent.

This stanza is the first in the poem to end with a comma. The sense continues into Stanza 24, and the consequent pausing and release of the rhythm gives a sense of movement. The spark is passing.

24 Le vent se lève! . . . Il faut tenter de vivre!
   L'air immense ouvre et referme mon livre,
   La vague en poudre ose jaillir des rocs!
   Envolez-vous, pages tout éblouies!
   Rompez, vagues! Rompez d'eaux réjouies
   Ce toit tranquille où picoraient des focs!

The wind rises! Life calls to be attempted!
The boundless air opens and shuts my book,
Bravely the waves in powder from the rocks
Burst! Take to your wings, dazzled pages!
Break, waves! Break with delighted water
This peaceful roof where sails were pecking!

At the opening of the last verse, the wind rises. It is action, or
rather perhaps the link between mind and action, the will to
live, the mysterious 'spark' itself. There is a sense of limitless
possibilities in 'l'air immense': for the etymology of 'immense'
gives us the meaning 'immeasurable'. The poet's mind has still
a lingering regret for contemplation; for he says 'Il faut *tenter*
de vivre', and 'La vague *ose* jaillir des rocs'. That one must
'*attempt* to live' suggests in part reluctance, in part admission
of necessity, in part desire. There is a two-way process indic-
ated here: if the mind is stimulated to activity by the body ('le
vent se lève'), the body is in turn stimulated to activity by the
mind: 'tenter de vivre' indicates a volitional element.

In line 2, the book's flapping pages are not only a visual
image for the white-capped sea; they are also the book the poet
is writing, or the poem he is writing. Writing is a form of
action; hence, only at this point, having accepted action, may
he be able to commence his task (the air at *this* point opens his
book). This connects with the next line 'La vague en poudre
ose jaillir des rocs' [The wave dares to burst from the rocks in
powder] which, to all appearances a way of describing the
rough sea breaking over the rocks, is also a reference to Moses
in the desert striking water miraculously out of the rock. In a
general sense the idea of motion out of stillness is repeated, as
also that of life out of sterility; and in the particular sense in
which we can attach it to the composition of a poem, it is the
'événement pur' (what could be purer than miraculous water?)
which is both the poem and the phrases of the poem, and

which appears, miraculously it seems, out of the 'void', out of apparent stillness, silence and sterility. The phrase 'et referme mon livre' hardly contradicts this notion, for the call to action impels the poet to close his book, symbol of inaction and of contemplation—and, in so far as it is the poem he has been writing, a symbol of his preoccupations throughout the poem, the obsessive 'fixity' which he has now rejected.

The poem is finished, and can be sent on its way, now out of the power of its creator: 'Envolez-vous, pages tout éblouies!' And we have finished the poem, and can let it fall. The pages are 'éblouies' because they are 'éblouissantes' (dazzling), reflecting the dazzling light of the sun, and because they express the thoughts of the poet 'ébloui' by both sun and sea, and by all they stand for. Too much light dazzled the eyes: away with such dazzlement! away with Teste! 'Envolez-vous' represents thus a rejection of the reigning splendour in the poem in favour of action, and also the handing over of the poem to the public.

'Rompez, vagues!' occurs twice. The first time it is an appeal to the waves to break; the second, an appeal for them to break the tranquillity of the poem's initial scene. A last call to action, both physical and mental. A last acceptance too of the beauty and wildness of the literal sea, hence of the beauty of the phenomenal world. The 'doves' have gone: the absolute, silence, contemplation, sterility, immobility, are rejected. We are left with the literal picture of the tossing sea, the metaphorical picture of joy through life and through action.[39]

The resistance of the ordinary reader to the analysis of poetry is often strong and bitter. He claims that 'analysis destroys poetry'. He may of course be merely rationalizing from his own unwillingness to see poetry as poetry at all: for most readers seem to react to poems as to prose-with-a-rhythm. Or, if he is reading it as poetry, there may be an ingrained distaste for examining the sources of the emotion he obtains from it, in the fear that this emotion may be found to be without basis, for we are profoundly, emotionally (!), attached to our emotions: no man likes being told he is suffering from an infatuation. But it is, in the last resort, impossible to rebut the accusation that analysis may destroy poetry: after all, the only proof or disproof is personal experience, and it is exceedingly difficult to tell a man that the effect of something on his mind is other than he thinks it to be. Even Empson, at the end of 'Seven Types of Ambiguity', considers this problem, and admits that, yes, analysis *may* destroy. The only consolation for readers who think that it does so, is to advise them to forget this exegesis forthwith. If their resistance to analysis is really so deeply rooted, they may not find this too difficult.

But, consolation apart, may one say that one's personal experience does not agree with theirs? That to have analysed a poem, not as a single line of rational discourse, proceeding without apparent detour from A to Z, but as a tangled thread of mixed, and sometimes conflicting senses and overtones, improves the poem for us? For a mass of associations have been revealed, some of those very associations which, presumably, made us say when we first read the poem, 'I don't understand it, but it's beautiful.' But, in the process of revealing them, we make contact with still deeper associations, we are aware that we have not exhausted and cannot exhaust the sense of the poem. We touch, but the statue does not crumble: beauty is not skin-deep. Is this not perhaps the real motive for the ordinary reader's reluctance to examine? That he is dimly aware that if he did examine, he would be led into an unending maze of woodland paths where his mind, brought up to be rational, nurtured on simple meanings, would begin to cry out for a simple, tarmacadamed, straight main road?

In any case *le Cimetière marin* appears to, almost vocally, demand analysis. It contains, like most poetry, a rational meaning. But its deliberate obscurity makes it essential to at least sketch out the beginnings of an analysis before we can begin to comprehend that meaning. Hence the large number of commentaries on it. But since it is a poem, it is not right to treat it as a French colonel has done, and content oneself with 'translating it into verse' (the colonel meant, of course, prose-with-a-rhythm),[40] with treating it in fact as merely a prose statement, but in a foreign language, say, Bantu or Chinook. For why, if it is intended as prose, was it written as poetry? 'Plus un poème est conforme à la Poèsie, moins il peut se penser en prose sans périr. Résumer, mettre en prose un poème, c'est tout simplement méconnaître l'essence d'un art.' [The closer a poem comes to Poetry, the less it can be thought in prose without perishing. To paraphrase a poem, to put it into prose, is simply to misunderstand what is the essence of an art.][41] The moment one begins any kind of analysis, one is driven to analysing poetically. In short, the imagery of the poem is ambiguous, in a poetic sense; a commentary must take account of this ambiguity.

After which, one may return to the poem for enjoyment, and forget the commentary. It will have served to open up certain of the mental paths in this particular poetic woodland, and they will remain open, even if less consciously so. I must withdraw my modicum of consolation: it is not really possible to forget. But substitute another: *le Cimetière marin*, like all true poetry, is inexhaustible.

NOTES

1. Valéry, *Œuvres*, Vol. 1, p. 1503. See p. 86 of the present work.
2. In *La Genèse du* Cimetière marin. See Bibliography. Walzer also has his doubts.
3. In The Philosophy of Composition, pp. 318–28 of: *The Poems of Edgar Allan Poe*, ed. K. Campbell (New York 1962).
4. *Correspondence of Schiller & Goethe*, 18 March 1796, Spemann edition, vol. 1, p. 134.
5. This passage will be found on p. 88. But see my note (p. 96) upon this point.
6. See J. H. Ingram, *Life and Letters of Edgar Allan Poe* (London 1886), pp. 222–3. Ingram accepts that there is at least something in Buchanan Read's statement, and goes on to adduce evidence for this. See also the discussion of the genesis of Poe's poem in: *The Poems of Edgar Allan Poe*, ed. K. Campbell (New York 1962), pp. 250–2.
7. In *Form and Meaning in Valéry's* le Cimetière marin. See Bibliography.
8. Eliot: *On Poetry and Poets* (London: Faber 1957), p. 38. Austin also notes (op. cit.) that Mallarmé, in a letter to Henri Cazalis, talks of working desperately upon 'une insaisissable ouverture de mon poème *qui chante en moi*, mais que je ne puis noter.' (My italics. '. . . an elusive opening to my poem *that sings within me*, but that I am unable to note down.') And we can see a very similar experience to that of Valéry's described by Mallarmé in 'Le Démon de l'analogie' (*Œuvres complètes* ed. Pléiade (Paris: Gallimard 1945) p. 272): 'Je sortis de mon appartement avec la sensation propre d'une aile glissant sur les cordes d'un instrument, traînante et légère, que remplaça une voix prononçant les mots sur un ton descendant: "La Pénultième est morte", de façon que *La Pénultième* finit le vers et *Est morte* se détacha de la suspension fatidique plus inutilement en le vide de signification.' ['As I went out of my flat I was accompanied by the distinct sensation of a wing slipping languidly and delicately over the strings of an instrument: this sensation was replaced by the sound of a voice pronouncing, on a descending scale, the words: "The Penultimate

is dead", in such a way that *The Penultimate* came at the end of a line and *Is dead* detached itself from the fateful suspension more uselessly in the void of meaning.'] We do not need to discuss the sense of Mallarmé's final phrase: what is important for the argument is that here we see the mysterious appearance of a non-verbal figure, which in turn is mysteriously 'filled out' by precise words. It is interesting that it should be Mallarmé, that implacable enemy of chance, who reports such an experience.

9. Vol. I, pp. 1474–5, Cf. pp. 1338–9 and 1685–6.

10. Cf. vol. II p. 567: 'Il est remarquable que les conventions de la poésie régulière . . . imitent le *régime* monotone de la machine du corps vivant . . .' [It is remarkable that the conventions of regular verse . . . imitate the monotonous running of the machine of the living body . . .]

11. See p. 86. Yves Bonnefoy makes a quite extraordinary speculation of this kind, speaking again of a *ten-syllable line*, that of 'La Chanson de Roland': '. . . lui dont les quatre pieds initiaux engagent si fermement la conscience dans la stabilité d'un savoir, cependant que sa deuxième partie, dans son rythme ternaire infus, consent au temps humain par un acte de sympathie qui revient se fondre dans l'éternel.' (*Un Rêve fait à Mantoue* Mercure de France (Paris 1967)) ['(a line) whose first four syllables engage consciousnes so firmly in the stability of a knowledge, whilst its second part, in its innate ternary rhythm, consents to human time by an act of sympathy which in turn fuses with the eternal.'] These are so precisely the concerns of Valéry in *le Cimetière marin* that one imagines this poem may well have prompted Bonnefoy's speculation. But Bonnefoy, a poet himself, should have known better: he has not seen the distinction between particular rhythmic figures and general metrical frameworks; and one cannot take seriously statements that pretend to apply to particular instances when they could, with a minimum of ingenuity, be applied to any poem, to any metre, and depend upon purely arbitrary assertions about the mystic meaning of numbers.

12. Vol. I, pp. 1503–4. See p. 86 of this work.

13. For an excellent account of the working of these metaphoric terms, in more detail than I give here, see Weinberg's commentary (see Bibliography).

14. Vol. I, p. 1504. See p. 86.

15. Cf. phrases in ordinary speech like 'Voyons' (Let's see), and 'Je te vois venir' (I see what you're getting at).

16. Vol. I, p. 1213.

17. Vol. II, pp. 231–4.

18. Vol. I, p. 1353: Valéry's italics.

19. Vol. I, p. 1504. See p. 86 of the present book.

20. One might speculate that we groan when, in ordinary conversation, we are faced with a pun, because we *reject* both alternatives. But reading poetry involves a kind of acceptance of statements we would normally reject.

21. '῎εστιν ἡ νόησις νοήσεως νόησις.' (*Metaphysics* XII. 1074b)
22. *Georgics* I. 243.
23. Not that we know exactly what this means: probably, 'the strengthless heads of the dead'. *Odyssey* XI.29. Cf. *Iliad* XV.251.
24. *Mark* IX. 44.
25. 'Paul Valéry vivant', *Cahiers du sud*, (1946), p. 276.
26. Vol. II, p. 45.
27. Vol. I, p. 1506. See p. 90 of the present book.
28. Ibid.
29. Ibid.
30. J. Burnet, *Early Greek Philosophy*, (1930), p. 182.
31. Vol. I, p. 1506. See p. 90.
32. The nineteenth century French philosopher, Tannery, takes this view. He writes: 'Zénon n'a nullement nié le mouvement (ce n'est pas un sceptique), il a seulement affirmé son incompatibilité avec la croyance à la pluralité.' (*Pour l'Histoire de la Science Hellène,* pp. 248–9.) ['Zeno in no way denied movement (he was not a sceptic), he merely affirmed its incompatibility with a belief in plurality.']
33. Cf. the expression 'les flèches de la satire' [the darts of satire].
34. Cf. the lines 'Qui ne connaît, et qui ne les refuse,/Ce crâne vide et ce rire éternel!' which are half question, half exclamation, and for which Valéry has chosen the exclamation mark.
35. Vol. I, p. 1343 (cf. p. 1365).
36. Ibid.
37. See p. 90. That darkness and splendour are here said to be complementary reminds us of the lines: '. . . rendre la lumière/ Suppose d'ombre une morne moitié,' and raises the question, Are death and fixity inevitable when the absolute is reached or believed in? This is, perhaps, the basic assumption behind the poem's metaphoric structure.
38. Vol. II, p. 667.
39. The epigraph from Pindar 'Do not, my soul, seek immortal life, but exhaust the field of the possible' was used also by Camus for his *Mythe de Sisyphe* (1942). The concerns of both poem and essay are not dissimilar. Both discuss varieties of 'philosophical suicide', both conclude with a call to live as much as possible, and both are led to this conclusion through a rejection of absolutes and of death.
40. Colonel Godchot in *L'Effort clartéiste*, June 1933, and *Ma Revue*, July 1933. See also *Valéry vivant*, Cahiers du Sud, 1946, pp. 373–6.
41. Vol. I, p. 1503. See p. 85.

Au Sujet du Cimetière Marin

Je ne sais s'il est encore de mode d'élaborer longuement les poèmes,[1] de les tenir entre l'être et le non-être, suspendus devant le désir pendant des années; de cultiver le doute, le scrupule et les repentirs,—tellement qu'une œuvre toujours ressaisie et refondue prenne peu à peu l'importance secrète d'une entreprise de réforme de soi-même.

Cette manière de peu produire n'était pas rare, il y a quarante ans, chez les poètes et chez quelques prosateurs. Le temps ne comptait pas pour eux; ce qui est assez divin. Ni l'Idole du Beau, ni la superstition de l'Éternité littéraire n'étaient encore ruinées; et la croyance en la Postérité n'était pas toute abolie. Il existait une sorte d'*Ethique de la forme* qui conduisait au travail infini. Ceux qui s'y consacraient savaient bien que plus le labeur est grand, moindre est le nombre des personnes qui le conçoivent et l'apprécient; ils peinaient pour fort peu, —et comme saintement . . .

On s'éloigne par là des conditions 'naturelles' ou ingénues de la Littérature, et l'on vient insensiblement à confondre la composition d'un ouvrage de l'esprit, qui est chose *finie*, avec la vie de l'esprit même,—lequel est une puissance de transformation toujours en acte. On en arrive au travail pour le travail.[2] Aux yeux de ces amateurs d'inquiétude et de perfection, un ouvrage n'est jamais *achevé*,—mot qui pour eux n'a aucun sens, —mais *abandonné*; et cet abandon, qui le livre aux flammes ou au public (et qu'il soit l'effet de la lassitude ou de l'obligation de livrer), leur est une sorte d'*accident*, comparable à la rupture d'une réflexion, que la fatigue, le fâcheux, ou quelque sensation viennent rendre nulle.

On The Graveyard by the Sea

These remarks were written by Valéry as a preface to Gustave Cohen's *Essai d'explication du Cimetière marin* (1933).

I do not know if it is still fashionable to elaborate poems over a long period,[1] to keep them between being and non-being, held in suspense before desire, for long years at a time; to cultivate doubts, scruples and changes of heart—to such an extent that a work is constantly being returned to and recast, and little by little takes on the secret importance of an attempt at reforming one's own self.

This manner of producing but little was not unusual, forty years ago, among poets and some prose-writers. For them, time did not count; an attitude which approaches the divine. Neither the Idol of Beauty nor the superstition of Literary Eternity had yet been discredited; and belief in Posterity had not entirely vanished. There existed a sort of *Ethics of Form* which was conducive to infinite labour. Those who devoted themselves to it knew well that the greater the toil, the smaller the number of people who can imagine and appreciate it; they were labouring for a very few—and as if devoutly . . .

The result of such an attitude is that one moves away from the 'natural' or naïve conditions of Literature, and comes insensibly to confuse the composition of a work of the mind (which is a *finite* thing) with the life of the mind itself (which is a transformational force constantly in action). Thus one arrives at work for work's sake.[2] In the eyes of these devotees of disquiet and perfection, no work is ever *finished*—a word which has, for them, no sense—it is *abandoned*; and abandoning it, handing it over to the flames or to the public (whether out of weariness or an obligation to hand it over), is to them a sort of *accident*, as when a train of thought is interrupted by weariness, an importunate intruder, or by some sensation or other.

J'avais contracté ce mal, ce goût pervers de la reprise indéfinie, et cette complaisance pour l'état réversible des œuvres, à l'âge critique où se forme et se fixe l'homme intellectuel. Je les ai retrouvés dans toute leur force, quand, vers la cinquantaine, les circonstances ont fait que je me remisse à composer.[3] J'ai donc beaucoup vécu avec mes poèmes.[4] Pendant près de dix ans, ils ont été pour moi une occupation de durée indéterminée, —un exercice plutôt qu'une action, une recherche plutôt qu'une délivrance, une manœuvre de moi-même par moi-même plutôt qu'une préparation visant le public. Il me semble qu'ils m'ont appris plus d'une chose.

Je ne conseille pas cependant que l'on adopte ce système: je n'ai point qualité pour donner à qui que ce soit le moindre conseil, et je doute, d'ailleurs, qu'il convienne aux jeunes hommes d'une époque pressante, confuse, et sans perspective. Nous sommes dans un banc de brume . . .

Si j'ai parlé de cette longue intimité de quelque œuvre et d'un 'moi', ce n'était que pour donner une idée de la sensation très étrange que j'éprouvai, un matin, en Sorbonne, en écoutant M. Gustave Cohen développer *ex cathedra* une explication du *Cimetière marin*.

Ce que j'ai publié n'a jamais manqué de commentaires, et je ne puis me plaindre du moindre silence sur mes quelques écrits. Je suis accoutumé à être élucidé, disséqué, appauvri, enrichi, exalté et abîmé,—jusqu'à ne plus savoir moi-même *quel* je suis, ou de *qui* l'on parle;—mais ce n'est rien de lire ce qui s'imprime sur votre compte auprès de cette sensation singulière de s'entendre commenter à l'Université, devant le tableau noir, tout comme un auteur mort.

Les vivants, de mon temps, n'existaient pas pour la chaire; mais je ne trouve pas absolument mauvais qu'il n'en soit plus ainsi.

L'enseignement des Lettres en retire ce que l'enseignement de l'Histoire pourrait retirer de l'analyse du présent, —c'est-à-dire le soupçon ou le sentiment des *forces* qui engendrent les actes et les formes. Le passé n'est que le *lieu* des formes sans forces; c'est à nous de le fournir de vie et de nécessité, et de lui supposer nos passions et nos valeurs.[5]

I had contracted this disease, this perverse taste for recommencing indefinitely, this indulgence in the reversibility of works of art, at that critical age when a man's mind is shaped and set. I rediscovered them in all their strength when, at about the age of fifty, circumstances led me to begin writing again.[3] I have therefore lived a great deal with my poems.[4] For close on ten years they have been, for me, an occupation of indeterminate length—an exercise rather than an act, a search rather than a release, self manipulating self rather than a preparation designed for the public. It seems to me that they have taught me more things than one.

I am not, however, advising the adoption of this system: I am not qualified to give anyone the least advice, and besides, I doubt if it would suit the young men of a period that is urgent, confused, and without clear perspectives. We live in a bank of fog . . .

If I have spoken of this long intimacy between some work of art and some 'self' of mine, it was only so as to give an idea of the very strange sensation I experienced one morning at the Sorbonne, on hearing M. Gustave Cohen giving a commentary *ex cathedra* on 'The Graveyard by the Sea'.

What I have published has never lacked commentaries, and I cannot complain in the least of any silence over my few productions. I am used to being elucidated, dissected, impoverished, enriched, exalted and cast down—to the point that I myself no longer know *what* I am or *who* is being spoken of; but reading something which has been printed about one is as nothing compared to the singular sensation of hearing oneself commented on at the University, in front of the blackboard, just like a dead author.

In my days the living might as well not have existed, for the academic; but I do not find it entirely regrettable that times have changed.

The teaching of literature gains from this new situation what the teaching of history could gain from an analysis of the present—that is to say some sense or inkling of those *forces* which produce acts and forms. The past is no more than the province of forms without forces; it is for us to provide it with life and inevitability and credit it with our passions and our values.[5]

Je me sentais mon *Ombre* . . . Je me sentais une ombre capturée ; et, toutefois, je m'identifiais par moments à quelqu'un de ces étudiants qui suivaient, notaient et qui, de temps à autre, regardaient en souriant cette ombre dont leur maître, strophe par strophe, lisait et commentait le poème . . .

J'avoue qu'*en tant qu'étudiant,* je me trouvais peu de révérence pour le poète,—isolé, exposé, et gêné sur son banc. Ma présence était étrangement divisée entre plusieurs manières d'être là.

Parmi cette diversité de sensations et de réflexions qui me composaient cette heure de Sorbonne, la dominante était bien la sensation du contraste entre le souvenir de mon travail, qui se ravivait et la figure finie, l'ouvrage déterminé et arrêté auquel l'exégèse et l'analyse de M. Gustave Cohen s'appliquaient. C'était là ressentir comme notre *être* s'oppose à notre *paraître*. D'une part, mon poème étudié comme un fait accompli, révélant à l'examen de l'expert sa composition, ses intentions, ses moyens d'action, sa situation dans le système de l'histoire littéraire ; ses attaches, et l'état probable de l'esprit de son auteur . . . D'autre part, la mémoire de mes essais, de mes tâtonnements, des déchiffrements intérieurs, de ces illuminations verbales très impérieuses[6] qui imposent tout à coup une certaine combinaison de mots,—comme si tel groupe possédât je ne sais quelle force intrinsèque . . . j'allais dire: je ne sais quelle *volonté* d'existence, tout opposée à la 'liberte' ou au chaos de l'esprit, et qui peut quelquefois contraindre l'esprit à dévier de son dessein, et le poème à devenir tout autre qu'il n'allait être, et qu'on ne songeait qu'il dût être.

(On voit par là que la notion d'*Auteur* n'est pas simple: elle ne l'est qu'au *regard des tiers.*)

En écoutant M. Cohen lire les strophes de mon texte, et donner à chacune son sens fini et sa valeur de situation dans le développement, j'étais partagé entre le contentement de voir que les intentions et les expressions d'un poème réputé fort obscur étaient ici parfaitement entendues et exposées,—et le sentiment bizarre, presque pénible, auquel je viens de faire allusion. Je vais tenter de l'expliquer en quelques mots afin de compléter le commentaire d'un certain poème considéré

I felt like my own *Shade* . . . I felt I was a captive shade; and none the less I identified myself at times with one or other of those students listening, taking notes, and from time to time glancing with a smile at this shade whose poem their lecturer was reading and commenting on, verse by verse . . .

I must admit that, *in so far as I felt myself a student,* I experienced little reverence for the poet—sitting there isolated, exposed and embarrassed on his bench. My presence was strangely divided amongst several ways of being there.

Among these multifarious thoughts and feelings which, for me, made up this hour at the University, the main one was certainly a sense of contrast between the reviving memory of my labours upon the poem and the finished form, the determinate and static work in which M. Gustave Cohen's exegesis and analysis were being brought to bear. This was to feel how opposed to each other are our *being* and our *appearance*. On the one hand, my poem studied as a *fait accompli*, revealing to the expert's examination its composition, its intentions, its means of action, its position in the framework of literary history; its connexions, and the probable state of mind of its author . . . On the other hand, the memory of my experiments, my gropings, my inward decipherings, and of those highly imperious verbal illuminations[6] which suddenly impose upon one a certain combination of words—as if such a group possessed some sort of intrinsic power—I was about to say: some sort of *will* to exist, totally opposed to the 'freedom' or chaos of the mind, and which can sometimes compel the mind to deviate from its purpose, and the poem to become quite other than it was going to be, than one thought it would have to be.

(Here one sees that the notion 'author' is not simple: it is only so from the point of view of a *third party*.)

Listening to M. Cohen reading my verses, giving to each its finite sense and its positional value in the development, I was torn between pleasure at seeing that the intentions and expressions of a poem reputed to be most obscure were here perfectly understood and expounded—and the bizarre, almost painful feeling to which I have just alluded. I shall try to explain it in a few words so as to supplement the commentary of a certain poem considered as a *fact*, by a brief look at the circum-

comme un *fait*, par un aperçu des circonstances qui ont accompagné la génération de ce poème, ou de ce qu'il fut, quand il était à l'état de désir et de demande à moi-même.

Je n'interviens, d'ailleurs, que pour introduire, à la faveur (ou par le détour) d'un cas particulier, quelques remarques sur les rapports d'un poète avec son poème.

Il faut dire, d'abord, que le *Cimetière marin, tel qu'il est,* est *pour moi* le résultat de la *section* d'un travail intérieur par un événement fortuit. Une après-midi de l'an 1920, notre ami très regretté, Jacques Rivière, étant venu me faire visite, m'avait trouvé dans un 'état' de ce *Cimetière marin*, songeant à reprendre, à supprimer, à substituer, à intervenir çà et là...

Il n'eut de cesse qu'il n'obtînt de le lire; et l'ayant lu, qu'il ne le ravît. Rien n'est plus décisif que l'esprit d'un directeur de revue.

C'est ainsi que *par accident* fut fixée la figure de cet ouvrage. Il n'y a point de mon fait. Du reste, je ne puis en général revenir sur quoi que ce soit que j'aie écrit que je ne pense que j'en ferais tout autre chose si quelque intervention étrangère ou quelque circonstance quelconque n'avait rompu l'enchantement de ne pas en finir. Je n'aime que le travail du travail: les commencements m'ennuient, et je soupçonne perfectible tout ce qui vient du premier coup. Le spontané, même excellent, même séduisant, ne me semble jamais assez *mien*. Je ne dis pas que 'j'aie raison': je dis que je suis ainsi . . . Pas plus que la notion d'Auteur, celle du Moi n'est simple: un degré de conscience de plus oppose un nouveau *Même* à un nouvel *Autre*.[7]

La Littérature ne m'intéresse donc *profondément*[8] que dans la mesure où elle exerce l'esprit à certaines transformations, — celles dans lesquelles les propriétés excitantes du langage[9] jouent un rôle capital. Je puis, certes, me prendre à un livre, le lire et relire avec délices; mais il ne me possède jusqu'au fond que si j'y trouve les marques d'une pensée *de puissance équivalente à celle du langage même*.[10] La force de plier le verbe commun à des fins imprévues sans rompre les 'formes consacrées',[11] la capture et la réduction des choses difficiles à dire; et surtout,

stances which accompanied the genesis of this poem, or of what
it was at the stage of desire and self-questioning.

I am intervening, moreover, only so as to present, under the
pretext (or by the subterfuge) of a particular instance, some
remarks on a poet's relation to his poem.

In the first place it must be said that *le Cimetière marin, in the
form it now has,* is *from my point of view* the result of the *inter-
ruption* of an inward labour by a chance event. One afternoon
in the year 1920, our much lamented friend Jacques Rivière
had come to visit me and had found me in the midst of a 'stage'
of this same *Cimetière marin*, thinking of reworking, rejecting,
substituting, intervening here and there . . .

He would not rest till he had read it; and, having read it, till
he had carried it off. There is nothing more decisive than the
mind of a man who edits a review.

It is thus, *by accident*, that the form of this work came to be
fixed. It is none of my doing. Besides, I cannot in a general way
return to anything that I have written without thinking that I
would make it into something entirely different had some out-
side intervention or some circumstance or other not broken the
enchantment of never finishing with it. I like only working *upon*
work: beginnings bore me, and I suspect everything that comes
immediately of being capable of improvement. What is
spontaneous, even if it be excellent, even if it be captivating,
never seems sufficiently *my own*. I am not saying that 'I am
right' in this: I am saying that this is the way I am made . . .
The notion of the Self is no more simple than that of the Author:
a further degree of awareness confronts a new *Self* with a new
Other.[7]

Literature, therefore, does not interest me *profoundly*[8] except
in so far as it trains the mind in certain transformations — those
in which the stimulative properties of language play a vital
part.[9] I can, of course, be caught up in a book, can read and
re-read it with delight; but it never possesses me totally unless
I find in it the traces of a thought *whose power is equivalent to
that of language itself*.[10] The strength to bend the common
word to unforeseen ends without breaking the 'hallowed
forms';[11] the capture and conquest of things which are difficult

la conduite simultanée de la syntaxe, de l'harmonie et des idées
(qui est le problème de la plus pure poésie), sont à mes yeux
les objets suprêmes de notre art.

Cette manière de sentir est choquante, peut-être. Elle fait de la
'création' un moyen.[12] Elle conduit à des excès. Davantage,—
elle tend à corrompre le plaisir ingénu de *croire*, qui engendre le
plaisir ingénu de produire, et qui supporte toute lecture.

   Si l'auteur se connaît un peu trop, si le lecteur se fait actif,
que devient le plaisir, que devient la Littérature ?[13]

Cette échappée sur les difficultés qui peuvent naître entre la
'conscience de soi' et la coutume d'écrire expliquera sans
doute certains *parti pris* qui m'ont été quelquefois reprochés.
J'ai été blâmé, par exemple, d'avoir donné plusieurs textes du
même poème, et même contradictoires. Ce reproche m'est
peu intelligible, comme on peut s'y attendre, après ce que je
viens d'exposer. Au contraire, je serais tenté (si je suivais mon
sentiment) d'engager les poètes à produire, à la mode des
musiciens, une diversité de variantes ou de solutions du même
sujet. Rien ne me semblerait plus conforme à l'idée que j'aime
à me faire d'un poète et de la poésie.

Le poète, à mes yeux, se connaît à ses idoles et à ses libertés,
qui ne sont pas celles de la plupart. La poésie se distingue de
la prose pour n'avoir ni toutes les mêmes gênes, ni toutes les
mêmes licences que celle-ci.[14] L'essence de la prose est de périr,
—c'est-à-dire d'être 'comprise',—c'est-à-dire, d'être dissoute,
détruite sans retour, entièrement remplacée par l'image ou par
l'impulsion qu'elle signifie selon la convention du langage. Car
la prose sous-entend toujours l'univers de l'expérience et des
actes,—univers dans lequel,—ou *grâce auquel*,—nos perceptions
et nos actions ou émotions doivent finalement se correspondre
ou se répondre d'une seule manière,—*uniformément*. L'univers
pratique se réduit à un ensemble de *buts*. Tel but atteint, la
parole expire. Cet univers exclut l'ambiguïté, l'élimine; il
commande que l'on procède par les plus courts chemins, et il
étouffe au plus tôt les harmoniques de chaque événement qui
s'y produit à l'esprit.[15]

to say; and above all, the control at once of syntax, harmony and ideas (which is the problem of the purest poetry), are to my way of thinking the supreme purposes of our art.

This way of feeling may be upsetting to some. It makes a *means* out of 'creation'.[12] It leads to extremes. More—it tends to vitiate the naïve pleasure of *believing*, which is responsible for the naïve pleasure of producing, and is at the basis of all reading.

If the author knows himself a little too well, and if the reader turns active, what becomes of pleasure, what becomes of Literature ?[13]

This glimpse at the difficulties which can arise between 'self-awareness' and the habit of writing will no doubt explain certain *partis pris* with which I have sometimes been reproached. I have been blamed for example for giving several texts of the same poem, and contradictory ones at that. As one might expect after what I have just said, I find this criticism hard to understand. No, on the contrary, I should be tempted (if I followed my own inclination) to invite poets to produce, as musicians do, a number of variations on or solutions of the same subject. Nothing would impress me as being more consistent with the way I like to picture poets and poetry.

To my mind, the poet is known by his idols and by his liberties, which are not those of the majority. Poetry is distinguished from prose by the fact that it does not have entirely the same restrictions nor entirely the same freedoms.[14] The essence of prose is to perish—that is, to be 'understood'—that is, to be dissolved, irrevocably destroyed, totally replaced by the image or impulse that it signifies according to linguistic convention. For prose always implies the universe of acts and experience— a universe in which—or *thanks to* which—our perceptions, actions or emotions must in the last analysis correspond or relate to each other in a single way—*uniformly*. The practical universe amounts to a number of *ends*. When an end is achieved, speech dies. This universe excludes ambiguity, eliminates it; it instructs us to proceed by the shortest paths, and it stifles as rapidly as possible the overtones of each event that is presented to the mind.[15]

Mais la poésie exige ou suggère un 'Univers' bien différent:
univers de relations réciproques, analogue à l'univers des sons,
dans lequel naît et se meut la pensée musicale. Dans cet univers
poétique, la résonance l'emporte sur la causalité, et la 'forme',
loin de s'évanouir dans son effet, est comme *redemandée* par
lui.[16] L'Idée revendique sa voix.

(Il en résulte une différence *extrême* entre les moments
constructeurs de prose et les moments créateurs de poésie.)

Ainsi, dans l'art de la Danse, l'état du danseur (ou celui de
l'amateur de ballets), étant l'objet de cet art, les mouvements
et les déplacements des corps n'ont point de terme dans
l'*espace*,—point de but visible; point de *chose*, qui jointe les
annule; et il ne vient à l'esprit de personne d'imposer à des
actions chorégraphiques la loi des actes *non poétiques,* mais
utiles, qui est de s'effectuer *avec la plus grande économie de forces,*
et *selon les plus courts chemins.*

Cette comparaison peut faire sentir que la simplicité ni la clarté
ne sont des absolus dans la poésie,—où il est parfaitement
raisonnable,—et même nécessaire—de se maintenir dans une
condition aussi éloignée que possible de celle de la prose,—
quitte à perdre (sans trop de regrets) autant de lecteurs qu'il le
faut.

Voltaire a dit merveilleusement bien que 'la Poésie n'est faite
que de beaux détails'. Je ne dis autre chose. L'univers poétique
dont je parlais s'introduit par le nombre ou, plutôt, par la
densité des images, des figures, des consonances, dissonances,
par l'enchaînement des tours et des rythmes,—l'essentiel étant
d'éviter constamment ce qui reconduirait à la prose, soit en la
faisant regretter, soit en suivant exclusivement l'*idée* . . .

En somme, plus un poème est conforme à la Poésie, moins il
peut se penser en prose sans périr. Résumer, mettre en prose
un poème, c'est tout simplement méconnaître l'essence d'un
art. La nécessité poétique est inséparable de la forme sensible,
et les pensées énoncées ou suggérées par un texte de poème ne
sont pas du tout l'objet unique et capital du discours,—mais des
moyens qui concourent *également* avec les sons, les cadences, le
nombre et les ornements, à provoquer, à soutenir une certaine

But poetry demands or suggests a very different 'Universe': a universe of reciprocal relationships, analogous to the universe of sounds in which musical thought is born and moves. In this poetic universe, resonance is more important than causality, and the 'form', far from vanishing into its effect, is so to speak demanded by it *in return*.[16] The Idea insists upon its voice.

(From this there results an *extreme* difference between the constructive 'moments' of prose and the creative 'moments' of poetry.)

Thus, in the art of the dance, the state of the dancer (or of the ballet-goer) being the object of this art, the movements or displacements of bodies in the dance have no term in *space*— no visible object; no *thing* which, once achieved, cancels them out; and nobody would dream of imposing upon choreographic actions the law of *non-poetic* and *useful* acts, namely that their end should be achieved *with the greatest economy of forces*, and *by the shortest route*.

This illustration goes to show that simplicity and clarity are not absolutes in poetry—where it is perfectly *reasonable*—and even obligatory—to maintain a condition as distant as possible from that of prose—even if one loses (without too many regrets) as many readers as may be necessary.

Voltaire has aptly said that 'Poetry is nothing but beautiful details.' What I am saying is no different. The poetic universe of which I was speaking offers itself through the number, or rather, density of images, figures of speech, consonances, dissonances, and the sequence of phrases and rhythms—the essential thing being a constant avoidance of what would lead one back to prose, whether by making one regret its absence or by following the *idea* exclusively . . .

In short, the closer a poem comes to Poetry, the less it can be thought in prose without perishing. To paraphrase a poem, to put it into prose, is simply to misunderstand what is the essence of an art. Poetic necessity is inseparable from palpable form, and the thoughts stated or suggested by a poem's text are not at all the sole and vital object of speech—they are *means* which combine *equally* with the sounds, cadences, rhythm and ornaments, to produce and sustain a certain

tension ou exaltation, à engendrer en nous un *monde*—ou un *mode d'existence*—tout harmonique.[17]

Si donc l'on m'interroge; si l'on s'inquiète (comme il arrive, et parfois assez vivement) de ce que j'ai 'voulu dire'[18] dans tel poème, je réponds que je n'ai pas *voulu dire,* mais *voulu faire,* et que ce fut l'intention de *faire* qui *a voulu* ce que j'ai *dit* . . .

Quant au *Cimetière marin,* cette intention ne fut d'abord qu'une figure rythmique vide, ou remplie de syllabes vaines, qui me vint obséder quelque temps.[19] J'observai que cette figure était décasyllabique, et je me fis quelques réflexions sur ce type fort peu employé dans la poésie moderne; il me semblait pauvre et monotone. Il était peu de chose auprès de l'alexandrin,[20] que trois ou quatre générations de grands artistes ont prodigieusement élaboré. Le démon de la généralisation suggérait de tenter de porter ce *Dix* à la puissance du *Douze.* Il me proposa une certaine strophe de six vers et l'idée d'une *composition* fondée sur le nombre de ces strophes, et assurée par une diversité de tons et de fonctions à leur assigner. Entre les strophes, des contrastes ou des correspondances devaient être institués. Cette dernière condition exigea bientôt que le poème possible fût un monologue de 'moi', dans lequel les thèmes les plus simples et les plus constants de ma vie affective et intellectuelle, tels qu'ils s'étaient imposés à mon adolescence et associés à la mer et à la lumière d'un certain lieu des bords de la Méditerranée,[21] fussent appelés, tramés, opposés . . .

Tout ceci menait à la mort et touchait à la pensée pure. (Le vers choisi de dix syllabes a quelque rapport avec le vers dantesque.)

Il fallait que mon vers fût dense et fortement rythmé. Je savais que je m'orientais vers un monologue aussi personnel, mais aussi universel que je pourrais le construire. Le type de vers choisi, la forme adoptée pour les strophes me donnaient des conditions qui favorisaient certains 'mouvements', permettaient certains changements de ton, appelaient certain style . . .[22] Le *Cimetière marin* était *conçu.* Un assez long travail s'ensuivit.

Toutes les fois que je songe à l'art d'écrire (en vers ou en prose), le même 'idéal' se déclare à mon esprit. Le mythe de la

tension or exaltation, to engender in us a *world*—or a *mode of existence*—that is entirely harmonic.[17]

If I am questioned, then; if someone is perturbed (as people can be, and sometimes quite deeply) about what I 'wanted to say'[18] in such and such a poem, I reply that I did not *want to say*, but *wanted to do*, and that it was the intention of *doing* which *wanted* what I *said* . . .

In the case of *le Cimetière marin*, this intention was originally no more than a rhythmic pattern, empty, or rather filled with meaningless syllables, which came to obsess me for a time.[19] I observed that this pattern was decasyllabic, and I made a few reflections upon this type of verse, which is very little used in modern poetry; it seemed to me poor and monotonous. It was a poor thing beside the alexandrine,[20] that three or four generations of great artists have magnificently elaborated. The demon of generalization suggested one might attempt to raise this *Ten* to the power *Twelve*. It proposed a six line stanza and the notion of a *composition* based upon the number of these stanzas, and strengthened by a diversity of tones and functions to be assigned to them. Among the stanzas, contrasts or correspondences had to be established. This last condition soon demanded that the potential poem should be a monologue of 'myself', in which the simplest and most constant themes of my emotional and mental life, as they had imposed themselves on me in my youth and been associated with the sea and the light of a certain place on the shores of the Mediterranean,[21] should be called up, interwoven and contrasted . . .

All of which led directly to the subject of death and bordered upon pure thought. (The chosen line of ten syllables bears some relationship to the line of Dante.)

My line had to be dense and have a strong rhythm. I knew that I was moving towards a monologue as personal, but also as universal, as I could make it. The type of line chosen, the form adopted for the stanzas, gave me conditions which favoured certain 'movements', allowed certain changes of tone, called for a certain style . . .[22] *le Cimetière marin* was *conceived*. Quite a long period of work ensued.

Every time I consider the art of writing (in verse or in prose), the same 'ideal' presents itself to me. The myth of 'creation'

'création' nous séduit à vouloir faire quelque chose de rien. Je rêve donc que je trouve progressivement mon ouvrage à partir de pures conditions de forme, de plus en plus réfléchies,— précisées jusqu'au point qu'elles proposent ou imposent presque . . . un *sujet,*—ou du moins, une famille de sujets.

Observons que des conditions de forme précises ne sont autre que l'expression de l'intelligence et de la conscience que nous avons des *moyens* dont nous pouvons disposer, et de leur portée, comme de leurs limites et de leurs défauts. C'est pourquoi il m'arrive de me définir l'*écrivain* par une relation entre un certain 'esprit' et le Langage . . .

Mais je sais tout le chimérique de mon 'Idéal'.[23] La nature du langage se prête le moins du monde à des combinaisons suivies; et d'ailleurs la formation et les habitudes du lecteur moderne, auquel sa nourriture accoutumée d'incohérence et d'effets instantanés rend imperceptible toute recherche de structure, ne conseillent guère de se perdre si loin de lui . . .

Cependant la seule pensée de constructions de cette espèce demeure pour moi la plus *poétique* des idées: l'idée de composition.

Je m'arrête sur ce mot . . . Il me conduirait je ne sais à quelles longueurs. Rien ne m'a plus étonné chez les poètes et donné plus de regrets que le peu de recherche dans les compositions. Dans les lyriques les plus illustres, je ne trouve guère que des développements purement linéaires,—ou . . . délirants,[24]— c'est-à-dire qui procèdent de proche en proche, sans plus d'organisation successive que n'en montre une traînée de poudre sur quoi la flamme fuit. (Je ne parle pas des poèmes dans lesquels un récit domine, et la chronologie des événements intervient: ce sont des ouvrages mixtes; opéras, et non sonates ou symphonies.)

Mais mon étonnement ne dure que le temps de me souvenir de mes propres expériences et des difficultés presque décourageantes que j'ai rencontrées dans mes essais de *composer* dans l'ordre lyrique. C'est qu'ici le détail est à chaque instant d'importance essentielle, et que la prévision la plus belle et la plus savante doit composer avec l'incertitude des trouvailles. Dans l'univers lyrique, chaque moment doit consommer une alliance indéfinissable du sensible[25] et du significatif. Il en

beguiles us into wishing to make something out of nothing. I dream therefore that I discover my work progressively, commencing with pure conditions of form, reflected upon more and more deeply—defined to the point where they propose or almost impose a *subject*—or at least, a family of subjects.

Let us note that precise conditions of form are no more than the expression of the intelligence and the awareness that there are *means* at our disposal, awareness too of their implications, as also of their limits and deficiencies. Which is why it comes about that I myself define the *writer* by a relationship between a certain 'mind' and Language. . .

But I know just how delusory my 'Ideal' is.[23] The nature of language lends itself as little as may be to consistent combinations; and besides, the training and habits of the modern reader, whose customary fare of incoherence and instantaneous effects makes him incapable of perceiving any craftsmanship in structure, hardly encourage one to stray so far from him. . .

Merely to think, however, of constructions of this sort remains, for me, the most *poetic* of ideas: the idea of composition.

I linger upon this word . . . It could lead me to goodness knows what prolixities. Nothing in poets has surprised me more and given me more regrets than the rarity of craftsmanship in composition. In the most distinguished lyric poets, I hardly find anything but purely linear—or frenzied[24]—development—that is to say, development which proceeds from point to related point, with no more organization of sequence than a flame running along a trail of gunpowder. (I am not talking here of poems dominated by a narrative, and where the chronology of events interferes: these are hybrid works: operas, not sonatas or symphonies.)

But my astonishment lasts only till I remember my own experiences and the almost disheartening difficulties that I encountered in my attempts to *compose* in the lyric genre. For here detail is at every moment of essential importance, and the finest and most intelligent foresight has still to compromise with the uncertain element of the *trouvaille*. In the lyric universe, there must at every moment be consummated an indefinable union of the sensible[25] and of the meaningful. The

résulte que la composition est, en quelque manière, continue, et ne peut guère se cantonner dans un autre temps que celui de l'exécution. Il n'y a pas un temps pour le 'fond' et un temps de la 'forme'; et la composition en ce genre ne s'oppose pas seulement au désordre ou à la disproportion, mais à la *décomposition*. Si le sens et le son (ou si le fond et la forme) se peuvent aisément dissocier, le poème se *décompose*.

Conséquence capitale: les 'idées' qui figurent dans une œuvre poétique n'y jouent pas le même rôle, ne sont pas du tout des *valeurs de même espèce*, que les 'idées' de la prose.[26]

J'ai dit que le *Cimetière marin* s'était d'abord proposé à mon esprit sous les espèces d'une composition par strophes de six vers de dix syllabes. Ce parti pris m'a permis de distribuer assez facilement dans mon œuvre ce qu'elle devait contenir de sensible, d'affectif et d'abstrait pour suggérer, transportée dans l'univers poétique, la méditation d'un certain *moi*.

L'exigence des contrastes à produire et d'une sorte d'équilibre à observer entre les moments de ce *moi* m'a conduit (par exemple) à introduire en un point quelque rappel de philosophie. Les vers où paraissent les arguments fameux de Zénon d'Élée, —(mais, animés, brouillés, entraînés dans l'emportement de toute dialectique, comme tout un gréement par un coup brusque de bourrasque),—ont pour rôle de compenser, par une tonalité métaphysique, le sensuel et le 'trop humain' de strophes antécédentes; ils déterminent aussi plus précisément *la personne qui parle*,—un amateur d'abstractions—; ils opposent enfin à ce qui fut de spéculatif et de trop attentif en lui la puissance réflexe actuelle, dont le sursaut brise et dissipe un état de fixité sombre, et comme complémentaire de la splendeur régnante;—en même temps qu'elle bouleverse un ensemble de *jugements* sur toutes choses humaines, inhumaines et surhumaines. J'ai débauché les quelques images de Zénon à exprimer la rébellion contre la durée et l'acuité d'une méditation qui fait sentir trop cruellement l'écart entre l'*être* et le *connaître* que développe la conscience de la conscience. L'*âme* naïvement veut épuiser l'infini de l'Eléate.

—Mais je n'ai entendu prendre à la philosophie qu'un peu de sa *couleur*.[27]

result is that composition is, so to speak, continuous, and can hardly be located at any other time than that of its execution. There is not one time for 'content' and another for 'form'; and composition in this genre is opposed not only to disorder or disproportion but also to *decomposition*. If sound and sense (or form and content) can easily be dissociated, the poem *decomposes*.

A vital consequence of this: the 'ideas' which figure in a work of poetry do not play the same rôle, and are not *the same kind of currency* at all, as the 'ideas' in prose.[26]

I said that 'le Cimetière marin' had first suggested itself to me in the guise of a composition in stanzas of six decasyllabic lines. This initial basis made it quite easy for me to distribute through my work all that it had to contain in the way of the sensible, the emotional and the abstract, so as to suggest, transported into the poetic universe, a meditation by a certain 'self'.

Since I was obliged to produce contrasts and observe a sort of balance between the various moments of this 'self', I was led to introduce (for instance) a reminiscence of philosophy at one point. The lines where the famous arguments of Zeno of Elea appear (but enlivened, jumbled, carried along in the impetus given by any dialectic, like rigging under a sudden squall) are designed to compensate, by their metaphysical tone, for the sensuality and all too human note of the preceding stanzas; they also define more precisely *the person speaking*—a lover of abstractions; and finally they confront everything that had been speculative and over-attentive in him, with the immediate reflex force, whose impulse breaks and dissipates a state of dark fixity which had been so to speak complementary to the reigning splendour; at the same time as it overthrows a set of *judgments* on everything human, inhuman and super-human. I misapplied Zeno's few images in expressing a rebellion against the duration and stringency of a meditation which makes one perceive all too cruelly the gulf between *being* and *knowing* that is developed by consciousness of consciousness. The *soul* wishes, naïvely, to exhaust the Eleatic's infinite.

—But all I intended to take from philosophy was a little of its *colour*.[27]

Les remarques diverses qui précèdent peuvent donner une idée des réflexions d'un auteur en présence d'un commentaire de son œuvre. Il voit en elle ce qu'elle dût être, et ce qu'elle aurait pu être bien plus que ce qu'elle est. Quoi donc de plus intéressant pour lui que le résultat d'un examen scrupuleux et les impressions d'un regard étranger ? Ce n'est pas en moi que l'unité réelle de mon ouvrage se compose. J'ai écrit une 'partition',—mais je ne puis l'entendre qu'exécutée par l'âme et par l'esprit d'autrui.

C'est pourquoi le travail de M. Cohen, (abstraction faite des choses trop aimables pour moi qui s'y trouvent), m'est singulièrement précieux. Il a recherché mes intentions avec un soin et une méthode remarquables, appliqué à un texte contemporain la même science et la même précision qu'il a coutume de montrer dans ses savantes études d'histoire littéraire. Il a aussi bien retracé l'architecture de ce poème que relevé le détail,—signalé, par exemple, ces retours de termes qui révèlent les tendances, les fréquences caractéristiques d'un esprit. (Certains mots sonnent en nous entre tous les autres, comme des harmoniques de notre nature la plus profonde . . .) Enfin, je lui suis très reconnaissant de m'avoir si lucidement expliqué aux jeunes gens ses élèves.

Quant à l'interprétation de la *lettre*, je me suis déjà expliqué ailleurs sur ce point;[28] mais on n'y insistera jamais assez : *il n'y a pas de vrai sens d'un texte*. Pas d'autorité de l'auteur. Quoi qu'il ait *voulu dire*,[29] il a écrit ce qu'il a écrit. Une fois publié, un texte est comme un appareil dont chacun se peut servir à sa guise et selon ses moyens : il n'est pas sûr que le constructeur en use mieux qu'un autre. Du reste, s'il sait bien ce qu'il voulut faire, cette connaissance trouble toujours en lui la perception de ce qu'il a fait.

The various remarks above may give some idea of the reflexions of an author in the presence of a commentary on his work. He sees in the latter what it should have been, and what it could have been, much more clearly than what it is. What then could be more interesting for him than the result of a meticulous examination and the impressions gained from an alien viewpoint? It is not in myself that the real unity of my work is to be found. I have written a 'score'—but I can hear it only when it is performed by the mind and spirit of another.

This is why I particularly value M. Cohen's work (apart from those things in it which are all too flattering to myself). He has sought out my intentions with remarkable care and method, has applied to a contemporary text the same knowledge and the same precision that he is accustomed to show in his learned studies in literary history. He has delineated the architecture of this poem as clearly as he has plotted its detail— has pointed out, for instance, those repetitions of terms which reveal the tendencies, the characteristic frequencies of a mind. (Certain words are more resonant for us than any others, as if they were harmonics of our profoundest selves . . .) Finally, I am most grateful to him for having so lucidly explained me to the young people who are his pupils.

As to his interpretations of the *letter*, I have already explained my views on this elsewhere;[28] but one can never insist too much upon this point: *There is no such thing as 'the real meaning' of a text.* The author has no special authority. Whatever he may have *wanted to say*,[29] he has written what he has written. Once published, a text is, so to speak, a mechanism which everyone can use in his own way and as best he can: it is not certain that its constructor uses it better than the next man. Besides, if he really knows what he *wanted* to do, this knowledge always interferes with his perception of what he has *done*.

1. Valéry knows, of course, that it was not; for this essay was written at a time when the reigning poetic manner in France was Surrealist or Surrealist-influenced, and the spontaneous products of 'inspiration' and of the subconscious were greatly prized. But even Surrealism apart, there are few poets who have ever taken the intellectual control of the poet over his poem to the lengths that Valéry recommends in this essay. The most important thing here from Valéry's point of view, is that he is as usual rejecting 'inspiration' as a false god. '. . . Je trouvais indigne, et je le trouve encore, d'écrire par le seul enthousiasme. L' enthousiasme n'est pas un état d'âme d'écrivain.' (Vol. I, p. 1204) ['. . . I used to find it unworthy, and I still do so find it, to write out of enthusiasm alone. Enthusiasm is not a fit state of mind for a writer.'] Valéry places most emphasis on sheer hard mental work in writing poetry: this, at least, produces the *best* poems. It is evident why Valéry objected to Surrealism, which for instance presented the results of automatic writing as literary achievements—or rather, anti-literary, but at any rate worthy of being read. On the other hand, Valéry does not, at least in his second poetic period, condemn inspiration out of hand. Entirely conscious creation would be impossibly difficult, or just impossible. It is the poet's experience, he admits, that words, phrases, even whole lines, leap as if from nowhere into the awareness of the poet. To this extent, 'inspiration' still has an indispensable function to perform.

2. A deliberate echo of 'art for art's sake'. But Valéry's emphasis is not, as Gautier's was, on the created object valid only in a world of art, not justified by everyday values, but on the process of creation. Even the 'finished' poem becomes therefore a machine to recreate a mental process.

3. See Introduction §I.

4. Valéry 'lived with' *la Jeune Parque* from 1913 to 1917, and *le Cimetière marin*, begun when he was still working on this earlier poem, was not 'completed' until 1920 (and then 'by accident').

5. This attitude to past and present is no doubt connected with Valéry's over-riding interest in (*a*) the process of creation, (*b*) the mental processes involved in reading a creation. The poem exists

as a 'thing'; it is not however as a 'thing' that it is interesting, but as the product and stimulator of 'forces'.

6. Here, specifically, is the role of 'inspiration' in Valéry, an important and necessary, but not a dominating one.

7. He is referring here to his theories on the infinite divisibility of consciousness (see my commentary on the Zeno stanza of the *Cimetière marin*). One can look at oneself looking at oneself, and so on, ad infinitum. And each 'self' that one looks at is less essential than the 'self' that looks, hence is an 'Other'.

8. Valéry here, as usual, evinces an extraordinary detachment from his 'authorship'—a detachment unusual among writers, who, like Sartre's waiter defining himself as 'a waiter', tend to define themselves as 'writers'. This is not to say that Valéry did not enjoy his fame—only that he felt to some extent separate from it. His attitude is consistent with his modest refusal to claim prerogative as the sole valid interpreter of his own work (see later in this essay). He prefers to regard the poem *functionally*. It can be viewed, he says, in three ways: (1) from the point of view of its creator, (2) as an object (suited for measurement, analysis, etc.), (3) from the point of view of its reader. The second way of viewing it tends to be discounted by Valéry. A poem, exists, for him, only *in act:* it is a machine for producing a state of mind, or a variety of states of mind and feeling. Hence his modesty: the 'self' that produces the poem is not the normal 'self' of its producer, and the poem exists, in the world at large, only in so far as it is productive of the poetic mood in people reading it. Thus, literature exists only in interaction with a reader.

9. i.e. its suggestive powers, its ability to 'recreate' in the reader's mind.

10. This is to demand an extraordinary control over the elements of language, but also an extraordinary unity between the intention of the poem and the verbal means adopted. Now, if we define poetry as 'the utilization of all the potentialities of language' (musical, suggestive and significant), then, although this is not a Valéryan definition, it will serve to clarify his meaning: he is asking, in fact, for poets who push the potentialities of language as far as they will go.

11. This is a restatement of Valéry's famous demand that the poet should impose difficult formal conditions on himself. Hence, no free verse (though Eliot says this is formally difficult too). But, in its context here, we can see the reason for this demand: it is so as to utilize to the full the formal (and musical) capabilities of language.

12. Creation is a means to verbal discovery. But words convey thought and feeling: so that this must also be a discovery of ways of thinking and feeling.

13. Lurking behind this mild sarcasm is the suggestion that the best literature is one which requires readers to read actively, to achieve an understanding of 'things which are difficult to say'. They will no longer be able to 'forget themselves', to 'escape' into

a world of imagination. One is reminded of C.S.Lewis's twofold
distinction (in *An Experiment in Criticism*, Cambridge, 1961) of
ways of reading into (1) the escapist, (2) the re-creative. Such
writing as Valéry's forces us to read in way 2. And this is, no
doubt, one of the *purposes* of 'difficulty' in modern art.

14. If, for instance, the basic rhythms of traditional verse are a
restriction, the *use* of such rhythms is a freedom.

15. This suggests a possible explanation of Valéry's concept of
the 'poetic universe': the sense of words in poetry is not
classified, pigeonholed and tucked safely away; for the sense is in
the overtones, and cannot exist without them.

16. Thus, a musical thought cannot exist without its music: it is
not so much *in* the music; rather, it *is* the music. We are sent
back to the actual words of the poem, even though we think we
have 'understood' the meaning. 'Understanding' in poetry is
consequently not the same thing as in prose; and poems are not
statements in the normal sense.

17. It would almost appear that Valéry is less interested in sense,
and more in sound, than most poets. But this statement of his
does not discount meanings: it simply suggests that the senses of
the words of a poem interlock 'harmonically' as do the sounds,
i.e. in a way different from prose.

18. One would normally translate 'vouloir dire' as 'meant' or
'meant to say', but then Valéry's play on words would be lost.

19. There is not necessarily any specific verbal content in
a poetic mood: hence it can exist *before* it has words.

20. A twelve-syllable line, and the traditional metre of serious
poetry in France.

21. i.e. his birthplace, Sète.

22. Rather as Deryck Cooke has claimed (in *The Language of
Music* (Oxford 1959)) that certain phrases, rhythms and
sonorities in classical music suggest or even impose certain
moods, Valéry here seems to be claiming the same of certain
rhythms and sonorities in poetry.

23. Oddly enough, after all his eloquence about conceiving *le
Cimetière marin* out of pure conditions of form, Valéry appears
to doubt his own statements. The explanation, however, is that
he is here referring not to the initial crystallization of words
out of an obsessive rhythm (for which, see my comments on pp.
22–24), but to the difficulties of *elaborating* a poem, of building up
what he calls 'consistent combinations,' i.e. a structure of
interrelating images and sounds: here an ideal point of success
is clearly impossible to reach. (As we have seen, Valéry regarded
le Cimetière marin as in a sense unfinished.) The reason why
language does not lend itself to these 'consistent combinations',
is its variousness. It is noteworthy how often in these remarks
Valéry makes an overt or implied comparison with musical
composition; and it is clear from numerous texts that he envied
the musician the 'purity' of his medium. In 'Propos sur la poésie',
for instance, he observes that the musician 'se trouve . . . en

possession d'un ensemble parfait de moyens bien définis' ['finds
himself in possession of a perfect set of well-defined means']
(Vol. 1, p. 1367), whereas the poet has to deal with language,
'cette matière mouvante et trop impure; [il est] obligé de
spéculer sur le son et sur le sens tour à tour, de satisfaire non
seulement à l'harmonie, à la période musicale, mais encore à
des conditions intellectuelles variées: logique, grammaire, sujet
du poème, figures et ornements de tous ordres, sans compter les
règles conventionnelles.' ['that too impure and shifting material;
[he is] obliged to speculate about sound and sense in turn, to
satisfy not only harmony and the musical phrase, but also a
variety of intellectual conditions: logic, grammar, the poem's
subject, figures of speech and ornaments of all kinds, not to
mention the conventional rules.'] (Vol. 1, p. 1369; cf. pp. 1412–15).
This ideal, a quasi-musical ideal of composition, is a fine one
capable of producing the symphonic richness of texture and,
meaning that we have noted in *le Cimetière marin*. But
difficult it certainly is; and it is hardly surprising that Valéry
should find the perfect realization of it virtually impossible.

24. i.e. governed by inspiration.

25. 'Sensible' in the sense of capable of being felt: it is a pity not
to be able to write: 'of the feelingful and of the meaningful'.

26. i.e. meanings in a poem are linked not only on the level of
significance, but also through sound and form. This affects the
meaning of 'meaning in poetry.'

27. This passage is by no means luminous. The most important
point is that it is not the sense of this stanza, in a *philosophical*
way, but in a *poetic* way, that matters. But for observations on
this whole section of Valéry's remarks, see my commentary on
the Zeno stanza.

28. A reading of my Introduction §II should help to explain Valéry's
views on the matter of ambiguity, to which he is here referring.
There is no doubt an implied reproach to M. Cohen here for not
making sufficient allowance for complexities of meaning.

29. Or again, 'meant'.

BIBLIOGRAPHY I
First Editions of the Principal Collections of Valéry's Poetry

Album de Vers anciens 1890–1900: A. Monnier et Cie,
7 rue de l'Odéon, Paris VIe, in 'Les Cahiers des Amis des
Livres', cahier V; 1920.
La Jeune Parque: La Nouvelle Revue Française, Paris, 1917.
Charmes: La Nouvelle Revue Française, Paris, 1922.

Unless otherwise stated, all references to the writings of
Valéry in my text are to the following edition:
Œuvres, Paul Valéry: NRF, Bibliothèque de la Pléiade,
Paris, 1957/60 (In two volumes).

BIBLIOGRAPHY II
A Selection of Works & Commentaries on
'le Cimetière marin'

1928 *Alain:* 'Charmes', Gallimard. (New edition 1952)
1931 *Palgen*, Rudolf: 'le Cimetière marin von Paul Valéry,
      Versuch einer Deutung', Breslau, Trewendt und Granier.
1933 *Cohen*, Gustave: 'Essai d'explication du Cimetière marin',
      Gallimard. (New edition, Gallimard & De Visscher, 1946)
1947 *Douglas*, K. N.: Translations, English, Spanish, Italian &
      German, of Paul Valéry's 'Le Cimetière marin', 'Modern
      Language Quarterly', December.
      Macri, Oreste: Il cimetero marino di Paul Valéry, studio
      critico, Florence, Sansoni.
      Weinberg, Bernard: An Interpretation of Valéry's 'Cimetière
      marin', 'The Romanic Review', April. Reprinted in 'The
      Limits of Symbolism', Chicago University Press, 1966.
1953 *Austin*, L. J.: Paul Valéry compose 'le Cimetière marin',
      'Mercure de France', 1er avril & 1er mai.
      Austin, L. J.: La genèse du 'Cimetière marin', 'Cahiers de
      l'Association Internationale des Etudes Françaises', juillet.
      Scarfe, Francis: 'The Art of Paul Valéry', London.

1953 *Walzer*, Pierre-Olivier: 'La Poésie de Valéry', Geneva, Cailler.

1954 *Austin*, L.J., & *Mondor*, Henri: 'Le Cimetière marin', 2 vols., limited edition, Roissard, Grenoble.

1959 *Lawler*, James R.: Form and Meaning in Valéry's 'le Cimetière marin', Melbourne University Press.

1964 *Schmitz*, Alfred: 'Valéry et la Tentation de l'Absolu', Gembloux.